Evil, Madness, and Truth

Gerda's Story

By

Tony Fry

Evil, Madness, and Truth: Gerda's Story

By Tony Fry

This book first published 2024

Ethics International Press Ltd, UK

British Library Cataloguing in Publication Data

A catalogue record for this book is available from the British Library

Print Book ISBN: 978-1-80441-379-1

eBook ISBN: 978-1-80441-380-7

Contents

Author's Prologue vii

1: Now 13

2: Birth and the Death-World 15

3: The Letter 25

4: Living the Contradiction 37

5: True to Myself 47

6: About Hohenlychen 55

7: The Camp 64

8: The Trial 73

9: Impossible Relationships 80

10: The Study of Evil 87

11: Dialogues with the Living and the Dead 97

12: Conversations with the Psychos 106

13: The Day the World Turned 119

14: The Problem of the Limits 127

15: Leadership and Guilt 134

16: Voices of the Mind 140

17: Learning 148

18: The Good 153

19: The End 158

Acknowledgements 159

Research Notes 160

Author's Prologue

The story to be told is hybrid. It is a mix of fact and fiction, history and approachable philosophical thought. It begs understanding. It poses questions. It aims to be a compelling read. It has a history. Above all, it transgresses the spirit of the novel: it is didactical. This does not make it unique, but it does make it unusual. For the reader who wants to be captivated by a world that escapes reality it will disappoint. But for one who wants to better understand the dark side of the human condition, it has a lot to say – especially at this time when evil appears to be so manifest. So framed, what is presented invites serious reflection.

...

A long time ago I was a soldier, a military policeman. I was sent to a small garrison city in Northern Germany. It was home to two British regiments, one artillery, the other infantry, plus one Dutch infantry regiment. The Cold War was at its height. I was based at what was once a city prison, now functioning as a guard room, a base for soldiers on guard duty, a prison for minor offences with punishment up to twenty-eight days, and as a detention centre for soldiers awaiting court martial for major offences. Years later I discovered the significance of this prison in the story I am about to tell.

Fast-forward two years from my time in the garrison city. I am standing at a station waiting for a train. It will take me to Köln, where I will change to another train that will go to Ostend in Belgium. Here I will board a ferry to Dover and spend Christmas with family in Bristol after two more train journeys. The journey is long and boring, except for the leg to Köln. The train is very crowded, but not with its usual travellers. Almost every carriage is packed. Every seat is taken and the corridors are full of people standing, or sitting on bulging cardboard boxes tied with thin rope and heavy string, or on bundles of clothing or bedding. These people are thin, sad and mostly silent. Despair is palpable, as is the smell of sweat and urine. I know who these people are – they are from a displaced persons camp and are the unwanted social detritus from the war in Europe. They lack a nation, proof of identity and anything beyond what they are carrying. I know where they have come from, which is a camp not far from my city. These people are former prisoners from the Bergen-Belsen concentration camp that, until recently, existed nearby.

Belsen was liberated by British troops of the 7th Armoured Brigade. My father was in one of those troops. I have no idea if he was involved in the liberation. He never spoke about the war, but he was physically and mentally damaged by it. I remember my mother telling me that he threw his medals in the river.

I am in the train corridor, wedged between an old man wearing a dirty British Army greatcoat many sizes too big for him and a young woman with a baby held over her shoulder. Around half an hour into the journey the baby vomits green bile over the off-white mackintosh I am wearing. There is no way I will be able to get to the toilet to wash it off. It's a struggle to take the coat off and when I do, I roll open the carriage window and throw it out. The only exchange between me and the young woman is a shake of her head as she raises the hand of the arm holding the baby. I touch her shoulder and try to smile. The German Government has decided to close the displaced persons camps over a period. This is why these people are on the move, to who knows where.

This was the 1950s – a period of silence, shame and concealment that writers like W.G. Sebald were later to rage against. While the horror and the outrage of the Holocaust arrived in 1945 in the form of images, it took over a decade for its horror to be existentially articulated and given voice by a number of books. For me, three stand out: Elie Wiesel's *Night*, a memoir based on his experiences of the Holocaust in the Nazi concentration camps of Auschwitz and Buchenwald, published in translation in English in 1960; Primo Levi's *If This Is a Man / Survival in Auschwitz*, English translation 1959; and Hannah Arendt's *Eichmann in Jerusalem: A Report on the Banality of Evil* from 1963. Adolf Eichmann was

a member of the group who organised the Holocaust. After the war he
fled to Argentina, where he was tracked down by Israel's Institute for
Intelligence and Special Operations (Mossad). Mossad agents smuggled
him out of the country and took him to Israel, where he was tried for
war crimes. He was convicted and in June 1962, was hanged. The trial
got major global media coverage. Arendt's book was based on her
reporting of the trial for *The New Yorker* magazine. Her use of the term
"the banality of evil" has resonated ever since.

Just over a decade ago I was prompted to revisit these events. I was
contributing to a book on "design in history" and decided to write on
design and the Holocaust, whose orchestration, in design theory terms,
had a design intent, a designed organisational structure and a design
form delivering mass death. During the research for this contribution, I
looked at a lot of images, including those of camp guards. One in
particular stood out – a beautiful blonde young woman. She turned out
to be a monstrously cruel and brutal person, deemed by her accusers to
be evil. Her career and life, and the questions they posed, "inspired" the
writing of this book. Besides raising the issue of the relationship
between madness and evil, and the differences between them, questions
about the significant challenges involved in representing madness and
evil are provoked. The first issue I want to consider is this: How can we
think about evil in a way that does not turn it into an abstraction and
reduce it to an object of purely philosophical inquiry? And, on the other
hand, how can we avoid mobilising evil emotively as if its meaning
were obvious and clearly understood?

My response to these questions is to continually bring the meaning of
evil into doubt, and to cut across a sensibility that asserts: "I might not
be able to exactly describe what evil is, but I know it when I see it." The
concept of evil is debated within many discourses, not least those of
religion, philosophy and politics, and is accompanied by a huge
literature that ranges from ancient Greek, Chinese and Indian texts, to
those being produced in the present. There is no consensus. Some
thinkers believe that the concept of evil should be abandoned in favour

of more morally grounded terms like wrongdoing. They believe, like
Friedrich Nietzsche, that the term "evil" is dangerously emotive and
invites extreme responses. The counter view is that evil, in multiple
forms, is already deeply embedded in existing moral, theological and
political thought. One of the most forceful examples of this view comes
from the 18th century philosopher Immanuel Kant who believed that
anyone who lacked the will to be morally good was disposed toward
evil. In contrast, Hannah Arendt's more modern view, framed by her
experience of the Holocaust, was that evil is defined by the act of
stripping a human being of their humanity. This, as she understood,
and as the sociologist Zygmund Bauman confirmed, is not merely the
individual act of a malevolent other but is equally the effect of a
designed system and comprises many banal and seemingly innocuous
actions.

As the concept of evil is so ensconced in everyday language and within
many discourses, arguments about how to approach it are largely
abstract, as the means to reform its usage simply do not exist. In fact,
the embeddedness of evil in language has been reinforced in modern
times, not least by the public exposure of the horrors of the Holocaust.
What the use of the term evil in an inchoate way tries to express, and
what proposed alternatives fail to do, is to evoke an act of excessive
negation that exceeds merely doing wrong or causing harm based on ill
intent. Rather, evil resides both in the intent and the desired
consequences of an action. It may employ reason, but is not guided by
it. Instrumentally-reasoned action is underscored and directed by an
emotional and irrational desire to cause harm by the exercise of power
against a powerless other (human or non-human). The question then
arises: Is such action an act of sanity? After all, an insane act can result
from the departure of reason, or be advanced by it.

Any serious consideration of evil brings awareness of a schism between
discursive concepts, general usage of the term, and popular
perceptions, and this raises another question: How can we deal with the
problem of representation that evil poses, recognising that it is always

metaphorically circumscribed and unable to be defined in essence except in terms of unbounded excess?

 Considerable literary imagination and visual iconography of evil exist that veer between the dark and mysterious and the sensationalised and horrific. A genre of books and movies supports the latter view. Exorcisms, witchcraft, mass murder, extreme sadomasochist violence – a litany of representational tropes, often clichéd – are exploited and evoke evil intent and acts. They are generative of stereotypical characterisations and act to obscure actual or metaphorical understanding of what is communicated by the concept of evil. Fundamentally, the essence of what the term evil strives to name is an excess beyond representation, which cannot be grasped, but invites being sensed as a depthless ineffable unknowability that is all-consuming.

Against this backdrop, the intent of the narrative is to reveal a movement from an understanding of evil as a "given" to an understanding of it as something "constantly to be questioned". Gerda's life journey mirrors this passage from an idea of evil as an assumed object of fear that occupies her, to a condition of uncertainty about it. Her life is, in effect, a lived meditation on the nature of evil and its relationship to madness, as the two ideas and experiences touch and are touched by each other. She sees the journey as a meditation in search of the truth of her mother and of herself.

Tony Fry

1
Now

I've gathered my thoughts. I am sitting at my desk looking out the study window of my apartment in Celle, a small city in Northern Germany. I moved in a week ago. I will be spending most of my time in my study, which is actually just a corner of my living room. The space is adequate for my reduced library. I sold most of my books for a pitiful amount just before I left the United States, where I spent most of my life.

The window in front of my desk overlooks the back yard of my two-up, two down apartment block. Each unit has a small, fenced garden. Mine has the prize, a beautiful cherry tree. I will sow vegetables soon. I've done this for many years – I like physical activity. I like gardening. It's a source of pleasure, and the results are rewarding. There is something satisfying about eating what you grow.

Another part of my life is walking. It counters the sedentary nature of the rest of my day. I'm just a five-minute stroll away from the paths along the banks of the River Aller. In one direction I can walk for hours, in the other I'm twenty minutes from the centre of the city. The location is one reason why I chose the place. Celle is a well-preserved, small medieval city, with ancient buildings, cobbled streets, elegant parks and a Schloss, now a classical music venue. All this attracted me. Before coming here, I read how it survived World War Two totally unscathed. The population surrendered *en masse* to the advancing British troops at the end of the War and so avoided the city's destruction. Maybe all this sounds boring, but not to me. Boring is what I need.

Not far from my desk is a small table on which I have placed a battered leather suitcase I bought in a junk shop for three marks. It has travelled with me over the entire journey of my life. We both show signs of damage: mine inner, it outer. We both have carried secrets. The suitcase has no interesting or redeeming features, no notable patina. Rather, it just looks old, stained, scratched and neglected. It came into my life this way. Although worthless, there is nothing I value more. To see it comforts me, and always has. Against the odds we have both survived. This suitcase was, and is, the repository of so much of the historical material that set my destiny and carries my story.

I never expected or planned to come to Celle. But not long ago I had an irrepressible feeling that I had to be near where I was born, and the past that ruled my life. So here I am on a Strasse in Celle, which is wide, tree lined and quiet. Most of its houses are detached family homes. On fine days in the late afternoon, I can hear the sounds of children playing and people chatting in the street. Children have been a physical and emotional absence from my life. In my teens I made a decision never to become a mother. I will say why later. But somehow, and unexpectedly, the sound of these children in the street makes the absence painfully present; I hear them in my dreams. One night I awoke, and found that my pillow was wet. Yet I had no recollection of crying. I kept this door to my psychological self closed and locked for over sixty years.

There is nothing in the street that I will allow to make demands on me. I feel safe and am determined to stay so. I am, and will remain, unnoticed.

2
Birth and the Death-World

Many people have kind and loving mothers; the unlucky don't. Even so, almost nobody has a mother like mine. While we parted company just a few days after I was born, she nevertheless has been the dominant presence in my life. Since the age of twelve I have not spoken her name. Until that age I didn't even know of her existence. I was completely overwhelmed by the discovery and shame of who and what my mother was. Somehow casting her name into silence created its proper place of oblivion.

I have read horribly melodramatic articles and reports in which she was called the evillest woman of the twentieth century. Although this claim is sensationalistic and perhaps dubious, it's beyond doubt that she was a monstrous person. Others have told her story, and I have no intention of simply repeating those accounts. But unavoidably, in telling my story, I have to revisit hers. While it's true that she was absent, she touched my life forcefully, and in many unwanted ways. Her shadow fell over me and installed a deep fear within me. This fear ruled my life and played out across years of mental anguish and illness.

Apart from the acts of conception, gestation and birth she could lay no claim to the role of mother. I discovered that she did not even acknowledge my existence. She gave me nothing to belong to, no identity, nothing except the fear of becoming her. By any measure, she did not possess a single virtue. Her negativity was the powerful and all-directive force in my life. Yet I more than merely survived.

Though she was hanged in December 1945, public interest in her continued, and continues. There have been books, newspaper and magazine articles, plays, a really bad film, and even academic papers about her. Her life on the Internet has attracted and nourished a new generation of neo-Nazis.

Worst of all, after hunting down many photographs of my mother, every time I see myself in a mirror, I confront, and recoil from, the doppelganger looking back at me, no matter how hard I try not to. We look identical. For me the likeness is more than uncanny. For years, from my teens, viewing myself in the mirror and seeing that I looked the same as her was a spectre of terror. Without disfiguring myself I did everything I could to make myself look different. But what affected me most was the very nature of her existence and the fear that she, and it, infected me. Central to this fear was a fact that I believed was never disputed: she was evil. I became consumed by an inescapable question: Am I also evil?

As I said, I was twelve years old when I learnt who and what my mother was. At that time, her sister – the woman who, until that point, I believed was my mother – told me that my birth mother was dead. As a convicted Nazi, war criminal, member of the SS, and concentration camp guard, she was hanged. Even though I did not completely understand, I can't begin to find words for how it felt to receive this news. I said nothing, and my aunt walked away. Intuitively I knew that something had ended. My childhood was over and I would never be the same.

My aunt did not want to tell me more, but I did get a few scant details out of her. She told me my mother's career started at Ravensbrück concentration camp, had developed at Auschwitz and ended at Bergen-Belsen. I also discovered that my father, to whom she was not married, was also in the SS, and was an engineer working at Bergen-Belsen. Later I wondered what there was to engineer at Belsen – it had no gas chambers. The discovery of my parents' identities completely overwhelmed me. The words shock, confusion and anger get nowhere near registering how I felt. My existence fell into an abyss; it was as if everything I knew, felt and believed had been vaporised. At the moment of finding out that the person I thought to be my mother was, in fact, my mother's younger sister, I also felt abandoned. Why didn't she tell me earlier and gradually? I went to my room. I couldn't cry. I was empty and numb. Maybe an hour later my aunt came to see me and said that the news she had given me had to be "our secret." What she really meant was that she did not want anyone to know who she and I were. It did not take me long – maybe a week– to realise I had been dealt an act of violence.

Over several weeks and months, many questions arose. They kept coming for years. Why did my mother do what she did? Who was my father? What happened to him? How do I find out more? But two questions overshadowed all the rest: Who and what am I? And, am I going to become like my mother? Looking back, the more I discovered, the more these questions haunted me. In time I did get some answers.

Over the years many people, including a number of psychologists, told me that evil does not pass from one generation to another. It was easy for them to say. It was just their opinion. They could cite no evidence. I knew they were trying to allay my fear, but mostly I think I was just being fobbed off. Anyway, their views made not the slightest impression on me. In time I learnt that my parent's genes were their sole gift to me, my looks were their looks, my blood was their blood. At the time I said to myself, why not their evil also? As far as I was concerned, I could not escape from what was within me. That I had not done evil things was of no comfort. It felt as if I was fated to do something terrible. The evil within was simply awaiting its opportunity. So I existed, frightened of myself, in an ever-present cloud of doubt. The same questions haunted my waking and sleeping hours. What did not arrive was an answer to the question about what evil actually was.

To be able to tell my story, first I have to recount where and how I came into the world, and say more about my mother. I was born in Bergen-Belsen Concentration Camp. Officially, at the time, I did not exist. My birth was not registered, and only a few people knew about me. My birth was retrospectively recorded as having been on April 10, 1945. Because so many people's personal documents were destroyed by bombs, shelling and fire that consumed homes and offices where records of births, deaths and marriages were held, for a few years after the war it was not hard to get a birth certificate. All you needed was a letter from a priest, lawyer, postmaster, or other official person, with the document's details certified by a justice of the peace. I presume my aunt organised this. My Christian name was recorded as Gerda. We will come to the issue of this and my family name a little later.

My coming into the world and the first few days of my life are a mystery except for two things: shortly after I was born, Belsen was liberated by the British Army and so, on April 15, 1945, I was discovered by the liberating troops, and taken to a German hospital near the camp. It strikes me as ironic that this place that existed to save lives was situated almost next door to a place that was designed to bring about the degradation and destruction of human life. As far as I know my mother never acknowledged my existence to anyone, but there is evidence confirming that she gave birth to me. This came from the woman who delivered me, herself a camp guard, as well as several *kapos* who were present. *Kapos* were the prisoners who were used to control other prisoners, and who retained their position of privilege by being brutal. It seems I started out as an item of trash, nothing more than the unwanted and abandoned offspring of a depraved woman. While this is a stark judgement, it's true.

Eventually I discovered that on the day the British arrived and liberated the camp, my mother, the most senior of the *Aufseherin* (female camp guards), accompanied the camp commandant, Joseph Kramer, to meet the arriving troops at the camp gate. As soon as the British officer in command was told who they were, both were arrested. Apparently, at this moment, my mother told the arresting officer about me. Not long after, I was found in her room. She had pinned a note to the blanket in which I was wrapped. All that was on it was the address of her father and stepmother. I read a doctor's report, when doing research as a graduate student, that said it was decided that I was to be "protected by silence regarding the identity of my mother" – a silence my aunt broke on my twelfth birthday.

There is no record of my mother making any reference to me either before or after the day she abandoned me. She said nothing in letters to her sister, Helen, or to her father. The note on the blanket was all there was. Why her silence? Was it an act of refusal or disassociation? I have no idea. Notwithstanding the note, I felt that my existence was disavowed. In a place where life had no value, and where it was literally wasted, it seemed to me that I was just another object of waste. The only source of doubt was the note naming my maternal grandparents, but it lacked even the briefest of messages.

According to the records I discovered, I was collected from the hospital at three months of age by my grandfather and his wife. I was passed to them by a British medical officer rather than by a German member of the hospital staff. By this time the war was over. There was no documentary reference to my parents or a family name. I was simply known as Gerda, *das lager klienes kind* – the small camp child. I have no idea who gave me my recorded name. My grandparents took me to the family home in the small town of Wrechen in Mecklenburg-Vorpommern, a hundred kilometres or so east of Hamburg, in what was then the Russian sector, which in 1949 became the German Democratic Republic (East Germany). I discovered this, and other details, through research that was done on my mother soon after her death; this information included an interview with my aunt. While she would not talk to me about my mother, she eventually told me how we came to live in the United States.

I'm not sure how long I stayed with my grandparents, but it wasn't long. They were what would now be called dysfunctional, their lives wrecked by a decade of disasters, beginning in 1936 when my mother's father, a farm worker who also did contract milking, had a fling with a girl in the village. His wife found out and killed herself by drinking acid. He was left with four children to care for: two boys, one 15 and the other 17, and two girls of 14 and 11. He did what many men of his generation did – married a WWI war widow looking for support for herself and her four much younger children. It was not a happy home and things got worse.

Although my grandfather joined the Nazi Party in 1937, as did his sons, he was furious when his two daughters wanted to join the Hitler Youth "League of German Girls." My aunt said that my mother had an extremely strong attraction toward fascism and the League. There were fights about it every day. My mother's identification with Nazi ideology was intense and was one of the reasons why, at the age of 15, she sought and obtained a job at the Hohenlychen complex, a famous Nazi convalescent home near Berlin for members of the SS.

Accounts I later read about my mother's life said she was "an attractive and impressionable young woman captivated by being in the presence of powerful members of the SS." There were reports that she even had brief conversations with a few of the Nazi luminaries she served at the convalescent home. The records show that in 1942, at the age of 18, she was sent to work at Ravensbrück concentration camp at the direction of the SS doctor who was the director of Hohenlychen. Her fate was sealed by this act. She progressed through a number of menial positions, and then in March 1943 she was transferred to Auschwitz-Birkenau in Poland. By January 1945 she had worked in a number of "punishment commands" and was promoted and moved to Auschwitz camp number one, part of the camp complex. A key qualification for promotion was an ability to be extremely cruel. By March 1945 she managed to get a transfer to Bergen-Belsen to join her boyfriend, my father.

My mother's SS career produced a complete break with her father. Helen, when giving evidence at my mother's trial, remembered that the first time she returned home wearing the uniform of a concentration camp guard, her father beat her and physically threw her out of the house. That was the last time she went home. My aunt told me that my presence in the family home generated huge tension. Though some of the family regarded me as innocent, like all babies, others, including my grandfather, felt I was a child touched by Satan. As a result of the acrimony, Helen broke with the family and took me to Berlin. At the same time, she changed her family name to Schwab, the name of a friend from Wrechen who died in the bombing of Hamburg while working in the city as a nurse in a military hospital. As already stated, obtaining identity documents, including for a change of family name, was not an unknown practice just after the war. When I asked Helen about why she changed her name, I was told it was not just because of the stigma of her family name, or because my aunt got notoriety in the press when she gave evidence at my mother's trial. Instead, she said it was for my sake. In truth, it was for herself. Schwab is the name on my birth certificate.

My stay in Berlin with my aunt was short. The Russians, fuelled by hatred because of the many millions of their compatriots the Germans killed, were still on the rampage. It was not a nice place for a young and attractive woman, and Helen was just as striking as her older sister. The fact that she had a baby meant she was a bit safer, but not much. Plenty of young mothers were raped. Times were hard, food was scarce and life was cheap. I'm not sure where or how, but she met an American army engineer who was being sent to Dusseldorf to disassemble machinery for optical instruments intended for the US. Apparently, we got a ride with him and he helped her get a job in the kitchens on the base where he was stationed. Again, this was not a history that she would talk about. What I realised was that she was a survivor and did what she had to do for both of us.

By the time I was three, Helen had a job in a US PX store on the base. She had a small apartment, an American boyfriend, a story about being a war widow, and an endless supply of chocolates, powdered eggs and potatoes. I still love chocolate and hate powdered eggs and potatoes. By the start of 1950, when I was enrolled in school, we were in San Diego, California. Helen was married to Marvin, the GI she met. He was now an electrician at the navy dockyard, and she was in the advanced stages of pregnancy. On 17 January 1951 she gave birth to Jason, and, fourteen months later, to another boy, Norman. Marvin never knew Helen was not my mother. Keeping him in the dark was part of "our secret."

When I learned of my circumstances as an adolescent, at first, I refused to believe most of what my aunt told me. Later I realised it was true, but Helen was selective. As a result, my emotional turmoil lasted years. It seemed as though I had an existence, but the reality of my life was unclear and might never be known. I wasn't certain of what was fact and what was fiction. Often in my teens I wanted to die.

Helen, after revealing the incomprehensible news in a flat mechanical kind of way, tried to assure me that everything would be all right, that I had a good life ahead of me, and that the past was the past. I knew that none of this was true. Instinctively I knew she didn't believe a word of what she was saying either. I now think that what she told me was really for herself, not me. She was offloading. She carried the burden of the lies of her life for a long time and suddenly she felt able to let some of it go. In dumping on me, she felt lighter. Whenever our conversations touched on our background during my high-school years, she repeated, "This is our secret, nobody else would understand. And remember, you need to keep your picture clear." I never worked out exactly what she meant by that. Anyway, the last thing I wanted to do was to share my heartache with someone else. Looking back, I have mixed feelings. Yes, I wanted to know, but Helen's way of telling me wasn't appropriate for anyone, let alone a child.

I realise that I was deeply affected by her rhetorical violence, even if it was unintended. I am now amazed that I mentally survived the trauma, albeit damaged. Maybe Helen needed help as much as I did. I have to say again, I believe the way she told me about my mother and her crimes was unforgivable. At the time, I didn't realise the harm being done by the insistence that I keep everything to myself. The experience led to clinical depression for which I eventually needed professional help.

I now understand that what stopped me from doing something stupid, what kept me alive, was my obsession with wanting to understand how the woman who was my mother could have done what she did. Were there connections between her and me, and would I end up being like her? So I deferred giving up on myself.

Of course, while what I have just said is true, it's a retrospective view. At the time, while I had clear questions that I wanted answers for, I mostly felt very confused. I certainly had no idea if being frightened of myself was abnormal. I'm pretty sure that by outward appearances, and from a distance, it looked as if I was growing up in an uneventful suburban family environment. We had an okay house, I went to an okay school, I was a good, if almost silent, student. We went on occasional trips in the family car. Superficially, it seemed as if we were just another middle-class family like the others in the street. We were not.

There were fault lines in the family structure. Aunt Helen and I were acting, Marvin was pretending all was well, and the boys were oblivious. As far as Helen was concerned, keeping up appearances was what mattered. Neither Helen nor Marvin were unkind to me, but neither were they aware of, or able to address, my hurt. Helen's own traumas prevented her from having any sympathy for mine so it was easier to sacrifice me in favour of her natural family. I recognised that, although she appeared to be warm and happy, she was not. She, like me, was emotionally damaged and sad, which I worked out years later.

The overwhelming picture I have of myself during this period of my childhood was of being alone in my bedroom. I read, did my homework, listened to music on an old second-hand radio I bought in a junk shop for three dollars. I also spent hours sitting at my bedroom window looking up and down the street. I watched people pass by, trying to read them, to work out if they also had dark secrets. What could I tell about these people's lives from their faces, how they walked and what they wore? Were these people happy, sad, tired, bored, lonely, sick, God-fearing, criminals? What could you actually discover from what people looked like? I thought about Mr Kennard who lived two doors away. He lived on his own, never had visitors, was very old and must have been hard of hearing as he seemed to spend all day listening to the sports channel on his radio at full volume. Could he be happy, and if he was, what could he possibly be happy about? Sport? Can listening to sports make anyone happy? Did he have a God, a wife who died, children who forgot him? Did he fight in the First World War? Was he just waiting to die? Was his face a mask, and if so, what did he hide behind it?

I didn't realise, at the time, how important questions of appearance would become for me. I wanted to believe what I saw to be true, but doubt always arrived. How do you know what is true unless you know what truth is? When I looked at Helen, I wanted to believe she loved me, and for a time when I was young, I thought she did. But after my twelfth birthday, I wondered. I was a belated and reluctantly-accepted duty bequeathed by her dead sister. Added to this was her absolute commitment to the image and idea she created of "the family." Inevitably, because of my history and the nature of my inner life, something was going to break, and it did. It happened when I was seventeen.

3
The Letter

In retrospect, having the mother I had meant it was not surprising that the fear and study of evil became a force directing my life. Although these ruminations were constantly with me, in actuality, as time went by, I discovered that reaching an understanding of evil would become increasingly elusive.

From the age twelve, through my teenage years and beyond, I either lay awake at night thinking frightening thoughts, or I slept in the land of nightmares. Sometimes I did both. Often, I woke myself with groaning or yelling, in a state of distress. I'm sure someone in the house must have heard me, but nobody ever came to my room or said anything in the morning. The images in my dreams came from visualisations arising from what I read about my mother. Concentration camps haunted me into adulthood. One recurring dream was of my mother hanging from a scaffold, her face purple, eyes bulging and a swollen tongue forcing itself out of her mouth. Another was of her, with whip and knife in hand, disfiguring the faces of young Jewish women.

Whereas most kids at my school went to the movies, swam, played baseball or tennis, watched football or went to the drug store for a soda or milkshake, I went to the library. I read everything on the Nazis I could find, even though most popular magazine articles about them were trash. No matter how bad it was, I made myself look. My preoccupation with the serious material started around 1958. By 1962 I had become an accomplished amateur Nazi hunter.

I was a good student and did well at school. By my own efforts I became a reasonable reader of German. By my mid-teens, I knew where a few important American and German war archives and collections were located, but I had yet to visit them. I learned how to find material from Ruth, a local librarian. She taught me how to make notes and record references. I started to fill notebooks. These were the days long before computers and the Internet, so the process of gathering material was slow. I sometimes waited for months for replies to letters, especially from overseas libraries: often none came.

 The research was done in secret, and I guarded my secrets. Ruth knew some of what I was trying to discover, but I was guarded. Secrecy was easy; nobody took any interest in what I was doing, and I kept my project to myself. I was very careful and organised. When I was fifteen, I acquired a post office box. All the mail was filed in a ring binder; my cuttings were pasted into scrapbooks and all my notebooks were numbered and dated. Together with a few books I bought, I kept these things locked in the old suitcase I've already mentioned. I kept it under my bed and wore its key around my neck.

As I grew older the gap between the family and myself widened, and especially the distance between Aunt Helen and myself. We were never close. One day, just after I turned fourteen, I said something to her in German and she totally freaked out. She pushed me against the kitchen wall, slapped my face and, talking between gritted teeth, told me never to speak to her in German again. I was shaken by the violence of her reaction. I looked over the top her head, said nothing, shrugged my shoulders, and walked off. Although I was really upset, I was damned if I would let her see my emotions.

The more strained things became at home, the more time I spent at the local library; it was my second home. Ruth became an important person in my life. She was a friend. As far as the family was concerned, I fit a pigeonhole labelled 'bookworm' and was a bit weird. That suited me fine. Once, when I was leaving the house, I bumped into Marvin as he returned from work, and he asked me where I was going. I said, "To the library." He replied: "Gee, I don't know why you bother when we've got a TV." I just smiled and walked on.

An area of research that became important over time was the reports and media accounts of war crimes trials. Long before I was able to read the transcripts of my mother's trial, I discovered a report about it. What it told me was that she was tried, along with forty-five other war criminals, each of whom was accused of crimes contrary to the Geneva Convention of 1929. I read this report in a March 1946 edition of *Time* magazine that I found in an archive box in the library. It said the trial lasted for two months and was carried out under British military law in a court in Luneburg, a small city south of Hamburg. It went on to say that after being found guilty and sentenced to death my mother was taken to Hamelin prison to await hanging. I looked up Hamelin, on the Weser River fifty kilometres southwest of Hanover. I already knew she had been hanged but somehow the words on the page and picturing the place where it happened disturbed me. I cried that night, but why? Was it for the horror of what my mother did? Was it because I was connected to my mother's evil? Or was it that my mother was now real but had abandoned me? I never worked it out. I read the *Time* article only a few weeks after the "against the wall" incident with Helen, so maybe how I felt had something to do with that.

In the same week I read the article, I also read about letters written by my mother to her sister and her father shortly before her death. Both were presented by prosecutors as evidence in her trial. I really wanted to see them and thought that, if I was lucky, I might be able to find them. It took me eight months. With Ruth's help I got copies of published reproductions of both letters – they were in an article on my mother published by the German newspaper *Die Welt* in 1948. I found out much later that during this period the paper reported on the trials. At the time it had a pro-British editorial policy. Germany's turn against the horror of its own recent history was gathering momentum.

Although I thought the letters were interesting, at first I didn't think they were very revealing. But as I read them repeatedly and more carefully, I changed my mind. I realised that the style of her writing, especially to her father, was quite strange. It also became clear that the letters raised more questions than answers. One of the first things I noticed was that while the letter was addressed to her father and her stepmother, the stepmother was not mentioned. Everything she said was directed to her father. More importantly, I remembered having read that my mother left school at fourteen and was "not one for writing." So I thought it strange that the letters were well written. Did someone else have a hand in them? This raised an unanswerable question: if someone else was involved, who could it have been?

Next, it struck me that the letters did not seem to be from an estranged daughter: they sounded affectionate. I doubt if father and daughter had any contact since the day he beat her and threw her out of the house in her SS uniform. Without any sign of a change of heart, or acknowledgement of the violence of their last encounter, or utterance of forgiveness, she addressed him as her *"lieber papa."* It seemed out of character and weird. It did not ring true. Neither did her description of herself as a "young brave girl, with a pure German soul inherited from her dear dad." This language was totally at odds with the way she must have viewed him after his abuse and violence.

A few lines later, knowing some of the monstrous things she had done, there was more fuel for incredulity: "I will go into the unknown with a clear conscience and above all proudly." The literary flourishes of the letter could not be hers. I just couldn't imagine her saying or writing: "I refuse to let any trace of fear or despair enter my heart. Peace and a great strength have replaced them, and to them I cling. They will be my true companions until my death." This is not the voice of a semi-literate.

Finally, it is absurd that she could claim, as the letter asserts, that "her conscience was clear" and that she was simply doing her "duty for the Fatherland." A similar sentiment was expressed in her letter to Helen: "Don't be sad, for I am dying for my country." This equally stilted letter was also written in a prose that seems out of character. It said very little except for a reference to a court observer called Annette who she refers to as if she were a friend. Apparently, Annette made attempts to procure poison so that my mother could commit suicide.

There was not a shred of remorse detectable in either letter. Neither was there any expression of sorrow, or an apology. She just invited her father "not to be ashamed" of her, and to hold his head high and to claim and recognise that in her death an "injustice has been done, which in time will be dealt with." Last of all, but for me most importantly, neither letter mentioned me. This brick did not hit me until I read both letters a couple of times.

Reading this correspondence many times over many years, I hear my mother's delusional voice *as well as* that of a more educated person who formally or informally helped her. The last lines of the letter to her father, with its hint of vengeance, suggests that this person was a Nazi. Perhaps, either my mother or her helper hoped to soften the blow of her death for her father and sister. Seen in the context of what I was to discover later, the letters completely reinforce my view that she lived in a fantasy. The image I settled on was of some kind of sympathetic scribe translating her sentiments into readable prose, not realising that the letter was to convince herself, via a fictional relationship with her father and sister. Reflecting on such thoughts led me to ask myself yet another question, one that opened up a new avenue of inquiry: What is the difference between madness and evil? Is evil not just one form of madness? And does madness exonerate evil?

What I found hard to deal with was that when I looked at pictures of my mother, she was beautiful. I was back with a particular version of the problem of evil and the relation of truth and appearances: can evil be beautiful? Hollywood would say yes, the ancient Greeks would have said no. What prevented me from quickly dismissing this question was that I had looked at every possible image I could find of camp guards. Every one of them was visibly marked by the experience. Even the halfway attractive ones looked hard and cruel. The worst reminded me of photographs of inmates at mental institutions I had seen in books on the history of photography.

In contrast, I collected a lot of images of my mother: she looked completely unlike the other female camp guards. In some she looked angry, in others I saw tiredness and aggression, and in just one image (taken when she was in a prison cell), she looked lost, but in every image her beauty was evident and unmarked by the cruelty of her actions. The photographs taken during her trial by the court photographer were extraordinary. She appeared in some to be disinterested and bored, but in others she looked relaxed and "normal" and in one she even looked demure. When she arrived each day, with her hair groomed and her clothes clean and pressed, she looked as if she just came from behind the counter of a department store selling perfume, women's underwear or shoes. She glowed in the darkness of the courtroom. Most memorable among the images I found were a couple of professional portrait photographs taken in a studio when she was younger, which were stunning. The most interesting image was one taken in a prison yard shortly after her arrest. It was clear from the image, if only to me, that she had recently given birth. The woman was uncanny in every sense of the word. Her actions and appearance did not match. It was impossible to imagine this beautiful woman being the monster I knew her to be.

I have never stopped asking myself how it could be that this woman who did so many horrendous things was not visibly touched by her actions and their results. Nothing she did seemed to affect her. In none of the pictures did she look mad or evil. But as witnesses at her trial said in their evidence in various ways, the inhumanity of her actions surpassed that of all the other camp guards. The images over which I pored preyed on my mind for a long time. I might go to a movie and see an actress who looked a little like her and totally drift out of the image on the screen into a moment of unwelcome reflection. The same thing could happen if I was reading a magazine, or if I saw someone even vaguely like her on a bus. Obsessively trying to make sense of something that does not make sense feels, in itself, like a kind of madness.

Putting these images together with the letter to her father and her (ignored) stepmother, as well as the one to her sister, took me to another area of investigation – the idea that she was a self-constructed illusion – an impression that others corroborated after her death.

I knew that my mother simply did not see the world around her as others did. The evil of her madness, or the madness of her evil, was not merely a condition of inner life directing outward action but the locus of her existence. For her, the unhinged world she inhabited was her *normal*. It's important to understand that in saying this I am talking about a person who shot people on a whim, beat the weak and helpless to death, and reportedly underwent an orgasm while disfiguring recently-arrived young and beautiful female prisoners. This is also a person who had sexual relations at Auschwitz with prisoners.

What I discovered about my mother eventually took me beyond the simple conclusion that she was evil or mad or both in any generalised sense. I realised that she was both totally delusional and also, probably, what psychologists diagnose as a "class four sadist", which means deriving sexual gratification from killing. The combination of these characteristics indicates that she was a psychopath. My mother was a person who was totally egocentric, emotionally shallow, very impulsive, and lacked any sense at all of empathy, guilt or remorse for any of her actions.

In later years I deduced that my mediated encounter with my mother produced in me a condition of clinical depression and post-traumatic stress disorder (PTSD). First recognised in returning US soldiers from the Vietnam War, an understanding of PTSD as a mental illness was not fully developed until the mid-1970s. It is now recognised as a condition suffered by millions who fought in both the First and Second World Wars, and perhaps in all wars. In fact, any major trauma can produce it. The extent to which somebody is affected is linked to the complexity of their genetic disposition, state of mind, and frequency of exposure to traumatic events. One can expect almost everyone who has experienced severe trauma to display evident negative consequences in the form of PTSD.

My mother created PTSD in others rather than suffering from it herself. The trauma was folded into her being as her normality. What she witnessed was trauma as a structural condition of the everyday. Her lifeworld was the lived actuality of Hannah Arendt's designation of the Holocaust as "the banality of evil." It's hard to imagine anything worse than the events that occurred every day in places like Auschwitz and Bergen-Belsen. Such events were ones my mother not only witnessed but instigated and inflamed. To continually practise grossly dehumanising behaviour in such a setting produced conditions of inhumanity in both victim *and* perpetrator alike.

For all the knowledge I acquired there was a bridge I never crossed. Certainly, I gained and accepted explanatory accounts about who my mother was and what she did. But none of this meant that I understood and came to terms with what I knew. Above all, what I discovered made it even harder to live with my fears.

My SS father contributed to the genetic cocktail of vileness that made me. I have no words that can express what it was like to realise that I am not outside the horror that spawned me. Their genes are their cursed gift to me.

Realisation that I am the biological and psychological prisoner of my mother and father started to arrive when I was seventeen. I knew I could not escape from them biologically and maybe mentally. The problem was that I had no idea who they really were. My father, who I will say a little about later, was an almost total mystery.

For all that I read about my mother, she would always remain that stranger who, even as I recoiled in horror from her, I wanted to know. I anguished over question I could never ask, and so never get answered. Was I more than an item of biological trash to be dumped on her family as a reminder of her shame? Was there just the slightest skerrick of kindness or care in her? Against the totality of unkindness and hatred she amassed, would her feelings toward me, if she had any, have counted for anything? Why did knowing this matter, considering what

I read about her? The perplexities of these questions caused a breakdown. It was not total, but neither was it minor.

During my last year at school I worked especially hard to get the academic result I needed to get into a good university, so this stress may also have been a factor. Whatever the cause, I went over the edge for a while. I felt myself to be utterly alone, confronting a life to be lived in the unfathomable depths of an abyss. At the most basic level there were only two paths in front of me: one led to an endless journey of despair, the other took me to the other side of my obsession where I could create an alternative to living in the dark shadow of my mother. Three questions tormented me. I repeated them to myself every waking hour over and over for years. Am I, or will I become evil? Am I, or will I become mad? What kind of life will I live?

Depending on the answers that came to me as I researched at the library, I vacillated between two fates: a life of angst ending in suicide, or one of increasing mental disorder perhaps resulting in institutionalisation. As at other periods of my life, for weeks I lay awake at night crying. I spoke to almost nobody, and found it hard to eat and concentrate. Helen must have seen that something was wrong, but she said nothing and showed no concern. The only person who did notice was my school friend, Karen. She saw my distress and assumed it was a result of the pressure of schoolwork. She insisted that I go to see a doctor. I did, and she came with me, but I had no way of telling him what my problem was. Things went the way I expected. He said I was suffering from the "schoolgirl blues" and fobbed me off with a script for a low dose of Valium. We called in to a local Walgreens drugstore on the way home. I got the pills and took one. It made me feel worse.

 The only thing that the Valium changed was that I felt less in control. I took the pills to school the next day and sold them for twenty-five dollars. Somehow, I just about managed to function, though I saw no prospects other than a shit life or an equally shit death. I'm not sure I would have made it through that time without Karen. Before the trip to the doctor our friendship did not go much beyond the classroom and walking to school together. But after the visit, we somehow bonded. She did not do much. She just talked and cared. What she did not realise, and what I didn't tell her, was that nobody else did. Nothing was said, but knowing I was not totally alone helped a lot.

Gradually the darkness lifted, but not totally. In the end I concluded that I could only assuage the situation by pursuing more knowledge, no matter how hard it might be, or how strange it might seem to someone else. That was the only way to overcome the tyranny of my mother's shadow. I knew that it could not lead to anything that resembled a normal life; I also knew my fate was sealed from the day of my birth. Yet I was beginning to come to terms with furthering my pursuit. It was the only way I was going to have anything like a life of my own. Effectively I affirmed my life by arriving at yet another question, one thrown against the others that haunted me: could I actually transcend what I had been born as and into? I realised this question, itself, was a mark of progress. If I couldn't escape the darkness of my being, I could at least learn how to travel with it. As it turned out it took almost a lifetime to discover that it was the search for what I needed to know that gave my life its form, direction and meaning. Quite simply, curiosity, not least about myself, kept me alive.

The combination of my fear of what seemed fated, and my obsession to know and fight it, meant that for a long time I was mostly solitary. My inner life dominated. How could I possibly share my secrets, or my questions? Withdrawal was inevitable. It was the only way I could cope. My solitude suited the family who were distant and, at best, only superficially friendly – Helen even less. We ate together only occasionally as the TV displaced the dinner table and conversation. Breakfast was staggered, and was a DIY stand-up affair. My basic material needs were met, although looking back it seems weird, as if I were living as a recipient of charity almost like an unwanted poor relation in a Dickens novel. I was an appendage to the family rather than a member of it. They had their own space, and I had mine. I was never asked questions, and I never caused trouble. The only reaction I got to my school reports, which were always good, was: "Well done, brainbox." I worked hard, walked to school every day, no matter the weather, coped even when under considerable stress, and stayed out of their sight. Maybe twice a month I went to the movies. The only time I watched TV was when there was a major unavoidable event, like when the Russians launched Sputnik 1 in 1957, when the Berlin Wall was built in 1961, or when John F. Kennedy was assassinated in November 1963.

Apart from a few car trips we certainly didn't do things together, like go on vacations, or to concerts or picnics. After their infancy, the only time Jason and Norman showed any interest in me was when they had a problem with their homework. Marvin was fine in math but his knowledge of history and geography was non-existent, and he wasn't much of a writer either. Helen was cute: if the boys asked her anything, she said, "You'd better go up and ask brainbox – she will know the answer to that." I didn't realise until I was about sixteen that I had been used as cover for her, and not just in relation to the past in Germany. It was me who helped the boys to learn to read, but it was Helen who took the credit among her friends. She was not totally illiterate, but almost. She could write a shopping list, but that was about it. I never saw her read a book, and whenever she picked up a magazine, she just flicked through it looking at pictures. I don't think she ever tried to read a newspaper.

Marvin was a present-but-absent sort of guy. He either had his head under the hood of his beloved car, or played football in the garden with his kids, loudly, or lay sprawled in the living room across a bust-out leather sofa, beer in hand, shouting instructions at a football, baseball or basketball team. As for the kids, they were in a world of cartoons and keeping clean. Helen had a real thing about hygiene. Besides homework, the only time I had any contact with the boys after the age of six or seven was when I occasionally babysat for Marvin and Helen when they had a night out for a special occasion, or went to a party. Apart from a miserable allowance, this was my only source of income. Helen was out at least three evenings a week – she earned pin money running "ladies lingerie events" for a sleazy pyramid sales company. When she started doing this, I was about fifteen and it crossed my mind that I might have a problem with Marvin hitting on me, but he never did.

While my disposition to withdraw was mostly responsible for my isolation, Helen more than encouraged it. She would say, in my presence, things like: "Gerda doesn't like parties, do you honey?" or "You would rather stay home with your books than come to the beach, wouldn't you, Gerda?" Her most common remark was, "That's not your number, is it kiddo?" In the end she did not need to say anything. I was just ignored. I knew why. My absence maintained her fiction. I knew that where I came from was not in the script of the play she wanted to be in. I was an extra who could inadvertently ruin the scene. She also saw in my appearance something that caused her pain, something she did not want to confront – an image of my mother. All this sounds self-evident but it was not so at the time. My understanding of the situation arrived out of a mist.

4

Living the Contradiction

As I have been saying, I was terrified that I was, or would be, possessed by whatever my mother passed on to me. Stupidly, I pictured an evil gene as a tiny black dot at the centre of my brain. The sense of latent evil within me made me feel as if I had no control over my fate. For a long time, irrational thoughts told me that I was destined to become immune to reason, to lose my mind and then my life. Living in this condition of corrosive angst I could find no comfort, just momentary distractions. Then slowly something changed. I found music thanks to my radio It became an elemental force in the preservation of my life. While anxiety was omnipresent and lingering, the emotional space created by music delivered respite. I came to a realisation of something obvious that I should already have known: without joy in something, my life was in danger from itself.

Everything changed but nothing changed. I continued to withdraw from the world around me. Not only was I afraid of what I might be and become but also of other people discovering my cursed heritage. I felt I had such a terrible secret that I had to conceal it – if I didn't it would destroy me. At all costs I wanted to avoid questions about my past. At the same time, I didn't want to lie to people, or construct my past as a fiction, which is why I decided that solitude was my best and only option. Although I felt that I was now taking more control of my life, I knew that I was also fostering a mental condition of withdrawal that was dangerous, and this frightened me.

As I've said, my bedroom, which was where I spent a huge amount of time, was at the centre of my secret life. The room was modest in every way. The furniture comprised a bed with my case stowed under it, a small wardrobe, a desk with two drawers in which I kept my schoolbooks, and a chair on which stood, most important of all, my radio. It was permanently tuned to WX2B, the local jazz station. Finally, there was a small bamboo bedside table, and a lamp with a dented red handmade shade, a worn green patterned carpet covering most of the unpolished floorboards and green curtains which, before they faded, would have matched the colour of the carpet. Everything else in the room was off-white: the walls, ceiling, paintwork, and my bedspread and pillowcases. On the inside of my wardrobe I stuck pictures of Billie Holiday, Ella Fitzgerald, Charles Mingus, John Coltrane, and Chet Baker that I cut out of magazines. If anyone visited and looked at the room, which never happened, they would think it just looked boring, but I loved it. My room, not the house, was my home. Whenever I arrived or left, I locked the door. My doing this was never mentioned.

 I now realise that my isolation and retreat into the space of work and contemplation that my room afforded allowed me to create a sense that my life could have a purpose. But to make something of my life I knew I had to confront my fear rather than repress it. I also became aware that my situation wasn't just a matter of my birth, or my own making, but was a product of a kind of uncaring. I'm not completely clear when this understanding, which came slowly, was gained, but I think it mostly arrived after my breakdown. Around the same time, I realised that my self-imposed isolation had helped me but had to end. I needed to put effort into becoming at least partly social. This was not going to happen organically, so how was I to do it? I could only work with what was socially available, which ruled out the family. I had to talk more to Ruth and give more back to Karen.

Ruth was in her early thirties; she was kind and friendly. Although I knew something of her life, and I liked her, I actually only knew her superficially. When I continued seeking out German history in the 1930s and 40s, she asked me why I was so interested in "such a grim subject." I took a deep breath and told her that my mother was dead and had been "in the Holocaust." The comment was vague, ambiguous, but of course misleadingly true. Ruth said she was sorry to hear that, but didn't pry. I liked her for that. She told me she moved to San Diego earlier in the year when she got married. Her husband, a chemical engineer, got a job at APSD, a local plastics company. They both came from Kansas City. She loved living by the ocean and this was a great discovery for her. I was surprised at how open she was. It became easy to talk to her. Unsurprisingly, most of our conversations were about books – those she read, those I'd read and the ones she suggested I read.

She was especially helpful when I later got interested in psychology and philosophy. I was amazed by how much she knew. She was way ahead of my teachers. I thought maybe she had done courses at university, so I asked her. She told me that she had studied Freud and Jung, but nothing on philosophy, though she read some of her father's books, and had many conversations with him. He was a professor of philosophy at Kansas State.

The time I spent in the library after school, a couple of days a week, positively affected my life. There I found that I could take responsibility for my education and also discovered that I had a deep love for books. Above all I took pleasure in research. For me it wasn't academically dry and boring but more like being a detective. After all, I was researching a criminal. It gave me a thrill. As for school, I generally tried to join in. Sometimes it worked, sometimes it didn't. I just couldn't connect with most of the girls, who were into boys, clothes, make-up and pop stars.

For a long time, I walked to and from school with Karen, often in silence, it never meant distance. She only lived a block away. But the more effort I made, the more our friendship grew. Many decades later we're still friends. I broke the habit of silence. I started with short conversations mostly about what I was reading, and about school, but increasingly we talked about music, and when we did, she took off and I had trouble getting a word in edgeways. Her dad was a jazz musician and she was not only very keen on music but also talented. This was great – I learnt heaps from her, my taste got educated and as time passed, I got much closer to her.

I often went to her place at the weekend and we listened to new records that her dad bought and she was usually raving about. I already liked jazz but talking to Karen and her dad really opened up so much more for me. I longed for the day when I could afford to buy a record deck of my own. It was from that point on that jazz moved from being music that I liked to becoming an important part of my life. Not only did Helen and Marvin not share my taste in music but exposed their innate racism by disparagingly calling it "black noise." My old radio never had much volume but every now and again I heard a scream coming up the stairs, usually from Helen, telling me to "turn the goddamn black noise down."

The thing about being friends with Karen was, then and now, that when we talked she did seventy-five per cent of the talking, which was just fine with me. Once we got past the usual venting about things at school – shitty teachers, cool teachers, kids we liked, ones we didn't, exams, homework and sport (we both especially hated jerk footballers with big mouths and empty heads) – Karen got into her music groove, describing her dad's gigs and the latest piano piece she was working on. What she said about things like chords, major and minor keys, half tones and improvisation went over my head for a long time, but I learnt. Her piano teacher, who was a friend of her dad, taught classical and jazz piano. He knew Bill Evans and actually worked with him in 1955 in New York, just after Bill moved there from Louisiana after graduating from music school. Karen was very talented so it was no surprise when she got a place in the jazz program at the University of Indiana, which was, and is, a great school.

During summer, when school was out, we met once or twice a week at the Ace Milk Bar. It had a great jukebox of hit records from before rock music was all the rage. I remember it had artists like Peggy Lee, Duke Ellington, Julie London, Jo Stafford, Mario Lanza, and Edith Piaf. Nobody seemed to play the records except us and the old guy who owned the place. There were always a bunch of teenagers from a nearby boxing club hanging around outside drinking coke and chatting. They were always lippy. Karen was quite a looker – she was slim, had jet-black hair and a stunning face, and wonderful, dark brown eyes, in part due to her Mexican grandmother. She also had a quick wit and a fast mouth from which she breathed fire at the dumb sexist guys. Anything was fair game for a cutting remark: haircuts, size of their dicks, acne spots, clothes and impending brain damage. Their egos just shrivelled in front of her. Every time she did it, I wished I could do the same.

So, while I never acquired other friends, and stayed mostly in the space I created for myself, I now realise that Ruth and Karen, without ever knowing it, saved my life. While I remained withdrawn, and still lived with demons, I felt stronger having these two friends. I felt valued. But there was one problem I couldn't talk about, and didn't know how to talk about. I felt that if I revealed my background, they would be horrified and abandon me, even if they appeared to remain friendly. I so wished I could trust them with the truth, but I couldn't force myself to take the risk.

From spending all that time in the library, I knew there was a lot more information in the world on my mother, the camps and the people I was interested in. But I was unable to get to it. It drove me crazy. I couldn't feed my obsession enough information to placate it. Even with the help I was given by Ruth, and my improved research abilities, it was almost impossible to get anything but fragments of the material I discovered existed, which was mostly located in Germany and Britain.

In those days, unless you were at a university or worked in a government department, almost the only way to gain access to rare or obscure archival material was to have professional accreditation and to travel to those libraries that held it. All I could do, and did do, was spend a lot of time in the San Diego County Library and second-hand bookstores, plus writing numerous *letters* requesting copies of documents. Even so, very slowly, I gained a significant amount of information and a clearer, if still incomplete, picture of my mother and her twisted world.

I avidly perused collections of *Life, Time,* and *Newsweek* magazines, as well as a complete collection of the *San Diego Union Parade,* a magazine inserted into the local Sunday paper, plus *Picture Post*, a British photo-journalism publication I thought was excellent. I read anything and everything on the Nazis, the war and concentration camps. Then I started to work my way through microfilm records of *The New York Times* and *Washington Post*. There were, of course, lots of stories on the progress of the war, America's entry after Pearl Harbour, some amazing photographs, lots of human-interest stories, and a few accounts of the liberation of camps, exposing their horror to the world. Yet I discovered that, no matter the horror presented by popular published accounts, and in radio news and movie newsreels, the reality was worse.

I often found significant and interesting things in, what appeared to be, marginal stories. I read, for example, a *Der Spiegel* story that intrigued and touched me. It was about the German film star, Marlene Dietrich, who was profoundly anti-Nazi and left Germany in 1930. However, she concealed something surprising. She had an elder sister, Elizabeth, she was ashamed of. Her sister, whose married name was Will, and her husband, Georg, ran the canteen in the troop cinema at the Bergen-Belsen Camp where German soldiers and SS guards and officers watched films, which were approved by the Nazi propaganda minister Joseph Goebbels. The pair, who had a son, were not prosecuted as war criminals, although they had given war criminals sustenance. What the article made clear was that Marlene supported them, notwithstanding their politics and values, but went to great lengths to keep her relationship with them secret, not least in order to protect her reputation. In the same story there was a critical comment about the song that Marlene is most famous for, *Lili Marleen*. Originally it was a poem written in 1915 by a Hamburg schoolteacher. It became a song after German singer-songwriter Lale Anderson adopted and adapted the poem and recorded it in 1939. Anderson was extremely popular all over Europe, but it was Dietrich's 1944 recording that got the recognition and glory, despite her loathing of Germany.

Although I read far more serious and chilling press accounts of camp life, this story got to me because I imagined the two people whose union produced me being among the crowd of moviegoers. Contemplating this passing moment of their life gave me a true sense of the nature of a perverse everydayness wherein the normal and abnormal, the human and inhuman, the banal and the horrific were constantly fused. This brief moment of reflection was given new resonance when, in 1963, I read Hannah Arendt's newly published book, *Eichmann in Jerusalem: A Report on the Banality of Evil.*

In 1934, Adolf *Eichmann,* as a member of the *Sicherheitsdienst* ("Security Service" – the SS) was working in its central office in Berlin dealing Jewish affairs. By absolute compliance to the aims of regime his career advanced, this seen especially in his being appointed to direct the expulsion of Jews from the City of Vienna after Austria was annexed by Germany in 1938. But his major career achievement was to manage the deportation and transport of millions of Jews from Germany, and nations its armies had occupied, to death camps.

After Germany's defeat Eichmann was arrested by U.S. troops and placed in a prison camp, from which he escaped. For several years he lived in Germany with a false identity, but in 1958 he moved to, and settled in, Argentina. It was there that in May 1960 he was arrested by Mossad (the Israeli secret service) agents, and taken to Israel where he was tried for his war crimes. Arendt attended the Eichmann trial and reported it for the *New Yorker Magazine* – these reports being the basis of her book.

What Arendt *made clear was that Eichmann* was an average and uninteresting, and not especially smart person, who thought, spoke, and enacted the ideology of Nazi Party ideology and its policies (including at his trial). In her view, he did not in any way think independently, or on the basis of belief, but rather in a form of absolute compliance to party doctrine in order to progress his career. Like many war-criminals, in his defence he argued he just did what he was to ordered to do. It was ambition drove him rather than ideology.

Famously, Arendt's book introduced concept of the "banality of evil" to define character of the Holocaust as it was directed. What this meant was evil being inscribed into the constant application of banal rules, regulations, instructions, memos issued by the central office in Berlin – all compliantly enacted without question by people from the highest to the lowest level, and with terrible consequences. Eichmann was a product, contributing author, and in the end a victim of the horror of the banality of this system.

Many of the accounts I read reduced me to tears. I remember, for instance, a heart-rending transcript of a broadcast by journalist, Edward R. Murrow, from Buchenwald shortly after the camp was liberated. He spoke of inmates dying in large numbers on the very day they gained freedom. It wasn't just his observation of the level of suffering that was so powerful. The well of sadness overflowed for me on reading how, having endured years of suffering, inmates died shortly after being freed. In his conclusion Murrow struggled to communicate his feelings: "I pray you to believe what I have said about Buchenwald. I have reported what I saw and heard, but only part of it. For most of it, I have no words." The utterance of "no words" was so familiar. In our present age, Murrow's final comment reads as almost trite, but for myself, I still live in the silence of the unspeakable, of images beyond words.

Anyone who tries to make sense of the Holocaust discovers very quickly that it is beyond representation. For all the books written and all the movies made, this conclusion remains true. Yet, while there is nothing we can say that communicates the extent of the horror, in defence of its memory, we still have to speak. It was not just a crime against the Jews, gypsies, other races, homosexuals, political prisoners and "criminals", but a crime against the very essence of humanity itself. It was all the more shocking because it came from a nation deemed to be at the centre of modern civilisation. Even more tragically, rather than being the last act of obscenity, it became its model.

Regardless of what I have said about the impossibility of representation, there were books that reached me like no others. Elie

Wiesel's *Night* was one that had a huge and shattering impact. I was the first person to borrow the copy acquired by the school library, and I returned it baptised in tears. I eventually bought a copy. There are three comments about Wiesel's account that I want to share, which make clear why the book brought me closer to grasping the actual, not metaphorical, hell that Wiesel experienced. First, his mother and younger sister did not survive Auschwitz (his father did not survive either, but died in Buchenwald), but Wiesel's two older sisters, Hilda and Bea, did. Second, the book became significant for me because it tells of Elie's arrival at Auschwitz when he was fifteen years old. I read the book when I was fifteen. I wondered if his mother had met mine, and hoped not. Third, I learnt from Wiesel of the absolute, life-destroying error of blind faith which, for the Nazis, was in the superiority of the Aryan race. It provided the foundation upon which their reduction of the Other, as less than human, rested. For the Jews this blindness took the form of a misplaced faith in God, about which Wiesel tells an illuminating story.

Wiesel relates that a child was hanged, but whose body weight was not sufficient to deliver a quick death. Wiesel was in a group of men who were marching past the gallows on which this boy was still thrashing about on the end of a rope. A man turned and asked Wiesel, "Where is God"? To which Wiesel replied: "Where is He? Here he is hanging on the gallows." The book forged an enduring proximity between itself, myself, and Wiesel, who remained silent for a decade after his liberation. His book arrived as a finished work only after his experience passed through an extended period of reflective silence – a silence like my own, which I am breaking at this moment.

A year after Wiesel's *Night* was published, Primo Levi's *Survival at Auschwitz* arrived in the bookshops. This was another book that became important. What I slowly came to realise from Levi was that the Holocaust was not just about the excess of inhumanity that burgeoned in concentration camps, but rather it was about something larger: the nature of humanity itself. He discovered through his experience an unspeakable flaw in all of us which persists – the ease with which we can regress to the inhuman.

After reading Levi I delved into a clutch of academic books that took a more detached tone, such as *The Destruction of the European Jews* by the historian Raul Hilberg. Then I read *The Complete Black Book of Russian Jewry* – a collection of eyewitness testimonies, letters, diaries and other documents about Nazi atrocities against Jews in the camps, ghettoes, and towns of Eastern Europe, compiled by the Russians Ilya Ehrenburg and Vasily Grossman. The first edition appeared in Russian 1944 and then in English three years later. It was almost six hundred pages of detailed, often dense, information. It seemed peripheral, but when I read about the Nuremburg War Crimes Trials, I remembered that the Russian book had influence in informing the legal team. I then revisited it, reading more carefully and in full. I also examined several books on the Trials that were published not long after their conclusion. Again, my perspective shifted. At its most basic, I realised that what was on trial was not just war crimes, or even crimes against humanity, but war and humanity themselves.

5

True to Myself

In 1964 I left "home" never to return. I got a place at the University of California, San Francisco, to study philosophy and psychology. Helen and I exchanged birthday and Christmas cards including a note for a few years. The only person I had occasional contact with was Norman, who became a lawyer. His elder brother Jason was conscripted into the Marines and killed in Vietnam. My "family" vanished.

At breakfast on the day before I was due to leave for San Francisco, Aunt Helen said she would like to talk to me. This was the first time any kind of formal talk had been mooted since the day she told me about my mother. She suggested 10.30. I agreed, and wondered what was coming. What arrived was a conversation that stamped itself on my memory.

Helen opened by saying that, like her, I should put the past behind. She then said, "As far as I am concerned, my life started the day I arrived in America." My reaction was, "What about your family in Germany?" She replied, "I know nothing about them because for me they do not exist," then asked if I would like a coffee. Helen was edgy. I still had no idea where things were going. When I said, "Yes, I'd like coffee," she headed to the kitchen at great speed, knocking over a small stool *en route*, which I picked up. Clearly she was flustered, even though we just started. Making coffee was a time-out.

When she came back we sat in silence for a few moments. Then, with a flick of her head, she blurted, "I'm glad you're leaving. I'll feel free at last after you've gone." I wasn't sure how to respond, but before I could say anything she added, "I owed it to my sister to look after you but we were too different from each other." After this, rather than things getting relaxed, they got more tense. Again, I decided to say nothing but knew she hadn't finished. "Marvin and the boys feel the same way as me. In fact, Marvin thinks you're an arrogant Kraut." I knew I was not welcome in the house, but this was the first time it was made explicit. The days of tolerating my presence were over and I knew that after I left, I would never come back. I was the last sign of her past, the last trace of Deutschland. As for the "arrogant Kraut" comment, I think that it was her view, not Marvin's. I also knew she wanted me to react to her provocation so that her conscience would be clear. I didn't. I simply said I understood how she felt and thanked her and Marvin for providing me with support and a home over the years. I added that I would be leaving in the morning before breakfast. Without saying anything else, and without looking at me or drinking her coffee, she left the room. Within a couple of minutes, I heard the front door slam. I never saw Helen again.

I went to my room and started clearing things out and packing. Even though I was not close to any of these people, it hurt to know they didn't want me. I realised that not being close is one thing, but being completely alone and unwanted is another. The break with Helen was more brutal than I expected. I did not want to leave anything behind, but there were things I couldn't take with me. It then hit me just how much I would miss those things and the security of my room.

After I finished packing, I walked over to Karen's house. I had arranged to stop by to say my farewells. As soon as I arrived, I gave Karen and her Mom an account of what happened and asked Karen's mom if I could leave a few things – clothes, pictures, schoolbooks and my radio – in their garage. When I asked if she could help me bring them around, she said we could go immediately in the car, which we did, then she invited me for supper.

I left after supper. We spent most of the evening talking about the past and our hopes for the future, ending by agreeing to keep in touch. We did, but I never went back for my things. Until she reads these words, which one day I'm sure she will, Karen has no real inkling of who I am and how important her friendship was to me.

When I arrived at what had been my home all the lights were out. I went straight to my room. I lay in bed and cried tears of departure, not for the loss of a family to which I never really belonged, but for the end of my childhood. In the morning I left behind my door keys and a note saying goodbye and good luck to Jason and Norman. A chapter of my life had closed more quickly than I expected.

The bus trip to Frisco filled the day. It was mid-evening when I arrived at the college dorm. Actually, the trip was more than a long ride, it was another kind of journey, a mental one. I saw almost nothing. I had a seat at the back of the bus, which was crowded all the way. I sat there, mostly with my eyes closed, thinking. Somehow recent events made me confront myself more seriously, and in a new way that I was trying to make sense of. I still had all my old fears but they were beginning to be tempered by the historical and experiential knowledge I had acquired about myself. As I thought about my psychological relation with my mother, I realised I was doing so from a position of more critical distance. Emotion was being tempered by intellect. I told myself I was getting stronger and hoped I was right.

I knew that, by the norms of the society in which I lived, I was not obviously mad or evil. I never had any sense that I displayed qualities of either of these conditions. I had, however, accepted the fact that I was withdrawn, socially inept, and could possibly be clinically diagnosed as having a personality problem. Although I pushed the idea of the seed of evil endowed by my mother to the back of my mind, it still lurked there. I knew that late teens and early twenties was a high-risk period for the emergence of mental illness. For all my rationalisation, and emergent resilience, I still lived with doubts. I also wondered what effect the change in my way of life would have on me: becoming more thoughtful certainly was one of them.

While I had read quite a bit about madness, I still had no clear understanding of what exactly madness or evil were. There seemed to be large gaps between how mental disorders were defined and how the more general condition of madness appeared. How much was really known? Where were the lines dividing genetic factors, brain chemistry, environmental determinations, mind-altering substances and a damaged life? Evil seemed to be even less clear than madness, which implied a fusion between beliefs and morality. As far as I can remember, what I ended up thinking was that madness was mostly an interpretative designation of bizarre and irrational behaviour rather than any specific mental condition. Evil, likewise, could be viewed in a similar way, but perhaps was even more relative. It thus rested with value judgments that were based on a norm, or norms, of "the good." Yet in both cases an assumption existed which said there was an inner cause – a malady, malfunction, demon, latent or active. I was to learn that I got a lot wrong.

The original question I had lived with became more refined. I was no longer asking myself, "Am I mad and evil"? Rather, it was, "For all my apparent normality, does madness and evil remain latent within me?" Doubt was starting to displace pure fear. What followed from all my reflection and reading as a high school student was that I recognised my future life was going to have a strong intellectual character and, rather than taking me away from my obsession with my mother, I would have to find out more about her, and at a more substantial level.

Thinking about my mother's conduct, it seemed hard not to believe that she was intrinsically mad and evil. Could it be that her SS membership and the occupation it provided simply enabled her to realise and amplify her innate traits? Was this view right or wrong, or did the conditions into which she was placed simply produce these traits in a person who was extremely gullible? The latter view corresponds with the proposition that monsters are made not born. Moreover, as medical research has shown, if the qualities of a two-year-old were replicated in an adult they would appear to be a monster, so maybe some of us stay monsters. If so, most of us just get better at repressing and concealing this fact. Of course, I could not be certain as to what traits my mother displayed before she joined the SS, or what her strong attraction to the Nazi party denoted. Was it the uniform and the culture, or the ideology? Were there common denominators between my mother and other female camp guards? Can personality defects lead someone into evil? Questions like these kept arriving.

This plethora of issues frustrated and puzzled me. On top of these, others emerged when I arrived at university, including demons from the past, and having to face the fear of my own sexuality. So far in my life I either ignored, or recoiled, from sex. I was even terrified to touch myself. I was frightened of what a state of arousal might unleash. I was scared that I would discover that I had the same perverse sexual urges as my mother.

I am sure many of my fears were completely unfounded and could have been addressed had I sought professional advice, but I just didn't know how to tell another human being that I had a mother whom history classified as inhuman and evil. Reason could not solve my problem. Even if the sciences of mind and brain were more sophisticated at the time, it would not have made any difference. The fear of my mother in myself was still unreachably deep seated.

All the thoughts I had about myself – my sexuality, appearance, state of mind and fears – converged to make one decision absolutely crystal clear and final. I would never become a mother. In a way I knew this all along, but I never expressly confronted it. In this confrontation I discovered that grief could arrive before life as well as after death. I grieved for having been born, for what I was, and for what would never be.

Strange, but I still have a strong memory of the last hour of that bus journey to San Francisco. My thoughts turned to how I was going to make out at the university. I was excited by the prospect of more resources, more music and more work. I knew I had to find a better way of dealing with people than in the past, and with the fact that I had something to hide. At the same time, I did not want to invent myself as fiction. This was something my ersatz mother did. The loss of my token illusory family did not exactly make the situation easier. I realised that all I could do was try to work things out as situations arrived and unfolded. As a result of my break from the connections that came from Aunt Helen and which had enveloped my life until the day I left San Diego, I realised that fear has a human geography. You can learn how to traverse your fears as you negotiate with different people in different social settings. You can find out what to reveal and what not to reveal, and where you can and cannot go. But you can also still get lost.

Another reason why I vividly remember that last hour on the bus is because I was annoyed with myself. I had forgotten three things I'd intended to do, as a result of the traumatic parting from Helen. First, I planned to go down to the library and say goodbye to Ruth and thank her for being so kind to me. She knew I was about to leave town and why. I sent her a card on my arrival at UCSF. Secondly, there was something I needed to say to Helen, but didn't. So I wrote, telling her that, whatever the limitations of the home I grew up in, the life I had there was infinitely better than the one I would have had in Wrechen. I acknowledged that with gratitude. I told her that I knew why she did not want to remember the past, but also knew that no matter what she did, she would never be able to forget it. Although I did not like her, or the way I was treated, I wanted her to know that I would remain grateful for her saving me. It was not easy, but I tried to withhold judgment about the choices she made. Like me, she was trying to survive the history that determined our fate.

The third thing I forgot was significant but less important. I meant to tell Karen about an article I read in the library the week before, about the big jazz scene in Germany. By the 1950s jazz had taken off there; it was getting considerable radio airplay, and there were lots of clubs. The article said that jazz was being heard as the sound of freedom, as a reaction against Nazi hostility to modernity, and, because it was black-culture music, it flew in the face of racism. The music was also international. The article prompted me to spend time finding out more about this scene. Every now and again I sent Karen cuttings about what

I found, and she did the same for me. In time, most of what she sent was about her wonderful musical career.

My time at UCSF was pretty much as I expected it to be. Because I was so motivated, I worked a lot harder than almost all my peers; I had a miniscule social life. Academically, I did exceptionally well. Even though I got a lot out of my study of psychology, I drifted away from the subject and towards philosophy where I found another world in which to dwell: a world of ideas. What I focused on, in retrospect, was always likely to be my major preoccupation: the philosophy of evil. As it turned out, my philosophical interest provided not only a framework that allowed me to deal with both myself and my intellectual development, it also gave me a way to deal with other people, especially guys. On this issue, Karen had been a great teacher. Her way of dealing with boys taught me a lot. I learnt a form of conversation based on parody and it went like this: a boy would start – "Hi my name's Joe." "Hi Joe, I'm Gerda." "So where are you from, Gerda?" "San Diego. How about you Joe, where's your hometown?" "Mine's very sleepy Portland, Oregon. It's great to be here in a place where there's some real life. Portland's a nice place, but it's really quiet." "What program are you in Joe?" "Anthropology, I'm really very interested in Latin America, especially the Amazon, which is where I hope to end up doing fieldwork." "So, you're really good at learning languages, right?" "Besides the French I learnt at school, I haven't really tried yet." "What about you, Gerda?" "My area's philosophy, and I'm especially interested in evil." "Wow, heavy, why evil?" "Well, Joe, I was born in Germany in 1945 in the last days of the evilest time and place in modern history – that's why evil is the focus of my life." Mostly I got, "Gee that's really interesting. Nice to meet you, see you around." But occasionally I made a friend.

Although the chat lines got a bit more sophisticated, and even esoteric, as I climbed the academic ladder, the result, nine times out of ten, was the same with dates who tried to come on to me during my undergrad and postgrad careers. At times there were exceptions, and I met some who were interesting, and I had some really good conversations, particularly with Jewish men. At first, I went out with a few, but always kept them completely at bay sexually. This resulted, I think, in getting a reputation as a "cold fish." Inevitably, invitations for dates, which were infrequent anyway, completely stopped.

Learning from lessons past, I got really involved in music. This is where I made good friends. I went to gigs, and occasionally to parties. Music mostly shaped my social life, which centred around coffee shops and talking about music and swapping tracks. I liked the scene, primarily because the only history these people were interested in was music and your musical tastes. Because I built up some knowledge of German and Polish jazz, and the music of a few other central European nations, I gained a kind of musical identity. I loved people like Thomas Denko and took pleasure into switching people on to artists they had never heard of, and of whom they ended up becoming fans.

The other big part of my life that university enabled was research. I finally got to use resources that I had been trying to gain access to for years. Now, my drive to understand my mother, her milieu, and what made her what she was had no bounds. My obsession was intellectual and unstoppable. I was leading two lives that informed each other – the life of a student meeting institutional requirements, and the life of my project by adding important knowledge that increased my ability to unravel questions about my mother's life and world.

6

About Hohenlychen

Before my mother arrived at Ravensbrück concentration camp she worked at Hohenlychen, an ambiguously named institution variously called a hospital, sanatorium and convalescent home, located some seventy-five kilometres north of Berlin and adjacent to the ancient town of Lychen.

I discovered more about the place when I read over the transcript of the character evidence given by Helen at my mother's trial at Luneburg in 1945. Then I learnt more after reading the material I discovered at the Library of Congress as a postgrad researching the history of euthanasia policy in Germany prior to the Second World War. This research made me realise just how significant the experience of working at Hohenlychen had been in influencing my mother's destiny. The story of Hohenlychen, and its director is interesting, relevant and worth telling.

It was established as a tuberculosis sanatorium for poor adults and children in 1902. Over the years buildings were added and slowly both it and the town of Lychen developed into a health resort. Then, in 1933, there was a dramatic change when it was taken over by the Nazis and turned into a *vorbildliches Krankenhaus* – a model hospital (although it still retained the title of Sanatorium). As such it was placed under the direction of the man who was to become its notorious SS Medical Superintendent, Professor Dr Karl Gebhardt, who was a lifelong friend from school days of Heinrich Himmler, the Reichsfuhrer-SS, Chief of the German Police, Minister of the Interior, and Commander of the Wehrmacht Reserve Army. It was Himmler who controlled the concentration camps.

Gebhardt, was a strange, smart and, as we shall see, amazingly contradictory man who held many conflicting values. He was a long-time supporter of the Nazis' "life fit for life" euthanasia policy and ideology. This vile project was directed at the extermination of the physically sick, the "mad and bad," and all those who were deemed to be a financial drain upon the nation and a danger to the health of German society. The policy and its implementation are now seen to be the precursor to the technology and practices of "the final solution" for which Auschwitz has become synonymous.

What struck me about the institution and its practices and underpinning ideology, was that the very people who dreamt up the appalling and horrific schemes carried out there were the actual "mad and bad" – to such an extent that they created madness and badness as a contagion. I also realised just how easily reason can be made to stand upon a foundation of unreason and so be contaminated and thereafter deployed in the service of hatred, racism and an unconstrained lust for power.

I learnt that the initial euthanasia policy was actually conducted under a program called *Aktion T4*. T4 stood for a Berlin address: *Tiergartenstrasse 4*, which with tragic irony, was the address of the totally misnamed headquarters of the *Gemeinnützige Stiftung für Heil- und Anstaltspflege* (the Charitable Foundation for Curative and Institutional Care). During the course of this program, which commenced in 1939, doctors euthanised (murdered) tens of thousands of people deemed incurable (physically or mentally), as well as criminals, gypsies, and Jewish and non-Jewish concentration camp and work camp prisoners. In less than a year of operation, the program killed over 70,000 people in euthanasia centres, mostly attached to psychiatric hospitals, in Austria and Germany. All of this activity was known publicly and therefore became contentious.

On the one side of the argument were people like Dr Joseph Mayer, a professor of moral theology and euthanasia supporter at the University of Paderborn. He wrote a paper erroneously suggesting that the churches should not oppose such a program. The T4 program created media interest and this generated at lot of public protest. Many doctors and nurses, including some employed in the program, spoke out against it. There were also expressions of concern from people in local towns. They knew what was going on and the meaning of the smoke coming from the chimneys of the crematoria. Many families of victims doubted the details of death certificates they were provided with. People then started to withdraw their sick relatives from the hospitals, asylums and sanatoria and look after them in their homes. Conversely there were many members of the medical profession and members of the public who supported the inhumane actions taken by the Nazis.

By 1941 the picture had changed, but not ended. Significant numbers of the German public feared that badly wounded soldiers would be euthanised, and this made the practices of T4 untenable. However, the program had effectively done its job and provided a trial run for the gas chamber technology to be employed in Auschwitz-Birkenau (the killing centre of the Auschwitz complex) when it was constructed in 1942. One of the key and frightful lessons learnt from the T4 program was that its success depended on taking the activity of killing away from medics and placing it in the hands of Nazi-indoctrinated camp staff.

As I said, Gebhardt was a supporter of the euthanasia policy and the T4 program. Like many others at the time, he became radicalised by the way Germany was treated after its loss in the First World War. Gebhardt served in the war, was taken prisoner and held in a prisoner of war camp in Scotland. In 1923 he joined the *Feirkorps*, a proto-fascist paramilitary organisation. Then in 1933 he formally joined the Nazi Party. Exactly when Gebhardt abandoned the Hippocratic ethos and became a "doctor of death" is not clear.

As a friend and personal physician to Himmler, together with his connections to other Nazis in the higher echelons of the party, Gebhardt's career flourished. Through the opportunities he gained via his privileged position, combined with his undoubted medical talents, he acquired an international reputation, especially as one of the founding practitioners of sports medicine. His attainments in this field were recognised in 1936 when he was appointed as chief physician to the Berlin Olympic Games. As a result of gaining this position, the Hohenlychen hospital and sports clinic were designated as the centre for treatment of Games athletes who acquired sports injuries.

Prior to gaining a profile for such treatment the clinic already established a reputation for developing extremely progressive methods to rehabilitate wounded First World War veterans. A delegation from the British Legion visited the clinic in 1936 with the intent of establishing friendly relations with rehabilitated German soldiers. On returning to Britain, they reported that they were impressed with Gebhardt's ability to rehabilitate amputees, and that men who lost an arm or leg were brought back to a high level of fitness and activity. They saw these men playing football, boxing and doing field sports. Unfortunately, with his deeply unethical values, Dr Gebhardt was just as inclined to inflict pain and suffering as to relieve it.

By the end of the 1930s Hohenlychen moved into another phase of its "development" and became a special hospital for the Waffen SS, where decorated soldiers and senior Nazi leaders were treated and convalesced. The profile of the institution was also increased by Gebhardt's appointment in 1937 to the chair of orthopaedic surgery at the University of Berlin.

During the two years my mother worked at Hohenlychen as a nursing assistant she fell under the spell of the place. This was as a result of her proximity to powerful, and in some cases, at least in her eyes, glamorous men, some of whom she conversed with. But more than this, her exposure to seeing the ravages of war upon the human body, as the clinic increasingly treated casualties, had a profound impact. It's almost certain that this experience hardened her attitude toward those people deemed "enemies of the state." She no doubt became aware of the experiments on prisoners that, as we shall see, started to take place at Hohenlychen. These experiments not only presented her with another view of the human body in which it was made an object of expediency, but exposed her to a perverted culture that "normalised" abnormally dehumanising conduct.

My mother's Hohenlychen employment ended abruptly; her fall from grace was supposedly because she failed to be accepted for training as a nurse. There are indications that subsequent to leaving Hohenlychen, she spent a brief period working in a dairy. Soon after this casual employment she was sent by the labour office to work at Ravensbrück concentration camp.

Initially she worked as a telephonist, then in 1942 was recruited by the SS as a guard at what was to become the largest women's concentration camp in Germany. Her move to Ravensbrück was not surprising as the camp had direct connections to Hohenlychen, and Gebhardt. It's even possible that my mother came to his notice as an attractive, if menial, ward assistant employed in transporting victims from the camp to be used and abused in the Hohenlychen experimental "science" program. This program was officially designated as part of the German war effort.

What Gebhardt set out to explore in one of his experiments was the effect of sulphonamides (a range of drugs used in the treatment of wound infections). Rather than aiming to prove that they worked, he showed the reverse, in response to criticism for not using the drug to treat a seriously injured senior Nazi figure. In order to defend his reputation, he crossed a threshold into a domain of inhuman practices that eventuated in his being tried as a war criminal at the American Military Tribunal at Nuremberg in 1947. He was found guilty and executed on June 2, 1948.

Gebhardt's experiments were sickening, the stuff of nightmares (including mine). The sulphonamides trials he conducted used women from Ravensbrück, mostly young girls from the Polish resistance. He violently broke their bones and then infected their wounds in order to conduct his experiments. The women suffered excruciating pain from both their broken bones and their infections. This was to demonstrate that treatment by sulphonamides was ineffectual. Some of the girls survived, while others died of their induced medical conditions, but most of them were executed once their "services" were no longer required. In another similar project, in order to explore ways of treating battlefield casualties with gas gangrene wounds, he again used camp inmates to test his methods. Frequently this resulted in the victim's limbs being amputated. In actuality the hospital became a place of torture and ended up being listed as a concentration camp. Effectively it acted as an extension of Ravensbrück for Gerbhardt's assistant, Herta Oberheuser, in her capacity as Ravensbrück's head physician. She directed a team of doctors who were complicit in these activities.

As evidence at his trial made clear, not only did Gerbhardt carry out experiments on prisoners at Hohenlychen and from Ravensbrück, he also conducted them on Auschwitz inmates. He supervised the "work" of numerous other Nazi doctors in many other camps. His career effectively represented the tragic fall of a whole class of German medical professionals and thinkers. Among them were men and women who once used their knowledge and abilities constructively, but who then allowed their talents to be perverted to advance inhuman and destructive Nazi objectives.

I have dwelt on these issues not because they are contextually significant to my story but because they remain alive. They are not just from the past. For example, I remember not long ago reading an article in *The New York Times* on a controversial debate in medical ethics over the kinds of research situations like the ones described. What this ongoing debate centred on was the question of the ethical issue of using the "good" elements of medical research by Nazi doctors that came out of the bad contexts under which the research was conducted. The question here is: can information be ethically used even if discovered to have been acquired unethically? It is not necessary to go very far back in time prior to the twentieth century to discover that a great deal of the history of medicine is unsavoury.

After the war the Hohenlychen hospital was taken over by the Russians and continued as a military hospital until the late 1990s when it was abandoned.

Once my mother joined the SS (although women never gained full SS status) she, in common with all recruits, undertook a process of induction into the application of pain and cruelty. This was to harden (dehumanise) them. More than this, it was to give them a taste of the repressed sadistic "pleasures" their instructors asserted were elemental to all humans. Moreover, rather than acquiring a new personality by their induction into these practices, recruits were depersonalised. They were thus stamped, via their induction, into the dehumanised mould. In order to victimise others, they first had to be victims. For a few, the loss of self was perhaps welcomed. Maybe my mother was one such person. In their training, recruits were told that whatever they did in the camps would be done in the service of the State and for the advancement of the Nazi Party.

Much of the information on my mother's susceptibility to such indoctrination came out of the evidence Helen gave at the trial. She told the court that as a child her sister was meek and fearful and, if threatened, would run away. To have all traces of her weakness erased, and then to be given power, authority, and protection afforded by the "gift" of authority, with its uniform and weapons, was a massive gain. Suddenly she felt powerful and quickly discovered the pleasure of acting without reserve against the weak and powerless. This was not a matter of conscious or reflective thought and feeling, but simply action based on following her implanted pattern of conduct and perverted (evil and/or mad) latent disposition. Everything she did was indivisibly both an uninhibited indulgence, and the exercise of her duty on behalf of the Nazi Fatherland. There was no guilt, no empathy.

Becoming an oppressor may have felt like liberation that allowed her and others to give vent to all that they once repressed. Maybe this conduct was a regression into something which our species, the most dangerous of all animals, had once demonstrated in its genocidal beginning. Thinking about this reminded me of an article I read while researching the early period of our species. It pointed out that by our aggression we wiped out our gentler Neanderthal competitors (who as contemporary research has discovered, were just as intelligent as our species). In other words, the meek did not inherit the earth.

My mind wanders, questions arrive. Is it the case that to be evil is merely to revert back to a time when our animality was dominant? Can an animal be evil? Is an animal evil that teases and tortures its prey before killing it? Beyond constructed human values, is there anything (as is the case with pleasure or pain) that is evil? And what about humans who have lost their humanity? The answer to this last question was to be found in the camps in two forms: dehumanised guards and those who came to be known as *Muselmann*.

The term *Muselmann* is said to have originated at Auschwitz (and was based on the kneeling position of the weak who did not have the strength to hold their back straight, and fell forward, thus looking like a Muslim at prayer). It was used among concentration camp inmates to refer to those prisoners who were near death due to exhaustion, starvation, or falling into a state of total hopelessness. In this condition they had abandoned their humanity and became the walking dead and thus devoid of all values, hope and dignity.

The Nazis running the camps considered the *Muselmanner* as less than undesirable. During gas chamber selections, these victims were the first to be taken. A person at this stage had almost no chance for survival; he or she would not live for more than a few days or weeks. The *Muselmanner* were viewed as the living dead, the human made inhuman: a residual being in whom the human was no longer present. As such, they were viewed with contempt. Their lives were regarded as spent and their being was despised. One asks, what actually made a *Muselmann*? Was it hunger, cruelty, weakness, or mental breakdown? Were they somehow born flawed? Were they a product of all, or just some, deprivations or deficiencies? And could it be that the SS, just as dehumanised, were but another *Muselmann* variant? As I thought about this, I again realised how limited language is – there are things that we simply do not have words for.

I began to grasp, out of this kind of thinking, the difference between the monster and the monstrous. The monster was/is the human without constraint. Monsters are not always born criminally insane yet they are never fully in complete control of their actions. Equally, they are sometimes "damaged goods" that remain, alongside other inflictors of damage, able to be held to account. I view my mother as, perhaps, such a being. She was not created in a laboratory by a mad scientist but rather by a monstrous system that exacerbated already flawed beings. Here is a system conceived and populated by people who created material environments in which the monster is moulded and thereafter acts, without question, under instruction via memos, verbal orders, standing orders, and established and sanctioned conventions that are every bit a part of the system. It's not possible to read and think about this kind of history without it having some effect. Did it depress me? Yes. Did it steal my youth? Maybe, but an empty grave cannot be robbed. Did it age me? I am not sure how this question came to mind, or how I could answer it, yet I know the answer is yes. I looked in the mirror and saw something invisible.

7

The Camp

The more I learnt about my mother the more I felt I had to make sense of the time she spent at Ravensbrück, Auschwitz and Bergen-Belsen. What was the relation of these places to what she was and became? Doing this was more than a matter of just putting fragments of information together.

Although I would never get a clear picture, it was not until I was in a position to do serious research that I could gain more information. A lot of what I had was impressionistic. The key to progress was in large part working from the transcript of her trial, where fragments of information came from her, but mostly from those who gave evidence, including Helen. I also discovered a number of published reminisces by victims and transgressors. I only had two other choices if I wanted to fill in the gaps: I could gain more general knowledge of the culture of the camps, a culture countered by the modest efforts of some inmates who managed to nurture a remnant of humanity in the face of the horror surrounding them; and I could use my imagination to grasp some sense of that lost history wherein truth had died with witnesses or when records were consumed in flames by Nazis.

My starting point was my mother's childhood, which was mostly a mystery. Little could be discovered about her early years and adolescence. All I had were those recorded remarks Helen made at the trial. Reading them, it was obvious that she blatantly resisted saying anything of substance. Many of her comments were evasive, things like: "There is nothing to say, she was just a child, that's it." It was not until she was pressed by the prosecution that she presented the characterisation of her sister already mentioned – as being weak and fearful, with a history of being bullied. There is no way to know if this is true or not. Any impression of my mother and her sister leading an uneventful life does not sit well with the traumatic consequences on the family of their mother's suicide.

There are educational records that show my mother left school in 1938 at the age of 14 with a poor record of school performance. This was the same moment when, along with Helen, she joined the League of German Girls (*Bund Deutscher Mädel*) and became one of its fanatical supporters. As already indicated, this association caused a lot of friction with her father. Her allegiance to the organisation, and his resistance to it, obviously influenced his reaction to her joining the SS and her subsequent complete break from her dysfunctional family. Beyond her time at Hohenlychen, and during the period immediately after, I could find nothing more about her early life.

While I knew of her move to Ravensbrück, which was about twenty kilometres from Hohenlychen, my knowledge of the camp was slight. But a little basic research told me that the camp was built in 1938, to house women and children. Most of the prisoners were Polish, but there were also Jews from elsewhere. Most of these people perished after being sent to Auschwitz in the latter days of the war. The camp was staffed by 150 female guards. However, as mentioned earlier, besides being a place of confinement, the camp also served as a training centre for female SS camp guards, and some 4,000 "graduated" from it.

By the age of nineteen my mother not only progressed from telephonist to guard but was appointed as a supervisor and established her reputation as being both nasty and brutish. This was in 1943, the year that the Nazi onslaught against the Jews was at its height – a horror she embraced with maniacal enthusiasm. My mother's "attainments" at Ravensbrück were no doubt among the main reasons that, in March 1943, she was transferred to Auschwitz, where she was to become the second highest ranking, and perhaps the most feared, female guard in the camp. Amazingly, as a senior supervisor (*Oberaufseherin*) she was responsible for approximately 30,000 female Jewish prisoners. I had a hard time coming to terms with this fact. I was not much older than nineteen when I first read it. I could not imagine this not very smart and meek country girl becoming pathologically cruel and gaining power over the lives of so many women. Her appointment was not, of course, based on her having any ability to exercise responsibility or act with care, but the reverse: it was her ability to excel in the delivery of cruelty that propelled her career forward. Consequently, it was at Auschwitz that her reputation as a violent, psychopathic and sexually perverted inhuman being was fully and firmly established.

What vestige of humanity she had when she arrived, if there was any, was completely lost. There is a good deal of written evidence about her violence, some of it sexual, including her relationship with the most notorious of all German torturing doctors, Dr Mengele. She also participated with him in the selection of prisoners to be gassed. As will be recalled, her savage and malicious conduct, especially against young and attractive women, was perverse. More than this she also shot, disfigured, whipped and humiliated huge numbers of other women, and was responsible for the death of thousands. I had many troubled and sleepless nights reading explicit accounts of her actions. Anyone would find this material harrowing, but consider what it felt like visualising this behaviour being conducted by your own mother. Such feelings exceed the bounds of sorrow and grief. An ocean of tears, as well as many sleepless nights, threw me back into an abyss. I felt that this darkness would last an eternity. I was taken past the point of even seeing her as a monstrous being. Her vileness had no limit. I can equally say that while I learnt to live with the pain that accompanied this recognition, it remains unabated and constant. I have a place within me where it lives as a wound. In spite of all that I learnt and supposedly knew, I still came back to a series of questions that colonised me and that I have spent most of my life trying to answer. What was the relation between what was intrinsic to her flawed being *and* the evil manifestation of inhumanity into which she was inducted? What was it within her that disposed her toward becoming such a monster before or after her camp persona arrived? And then, was she anything but pure nothingness without this madness that occupied her?

Over the years I spent a huge amount of time looking at the photographs of my mother that I've mentioned. Rather than just seeing them as images, I treated them as objects of concealment that contained information I had to find a way to access. There were six images in particular that preoccupied me. The first was a slightly overexposed portrait snapshot taken when she was maybe 15. She looks relaxed and pretty, and the image is self-consciously posed. There is not a single sign that you are looking at an ill-educated young woman from rural Germany with an unhappy family. The second was another portrait taken just before her departure for Ravensbrück when she was 18. This one is a lit studio shot taken by a professional photographer or a very skilled amateur. She looks very glamorous and the incongruity between her past and her future is extreme. Number three was taken shortly after she was arrested in the yard of Celle prison. She was standing next to Bergen-Belsen Camp Commandant Kramer, with a British soldier standing behind them holding a Sten gun (there is also an image taken at the same time, with her in the same pose, but without Kramer or the soldier in the frame). I believe it to be a post-natal image – she looks heavier and her stomach is larger, compared with others taken before and after where she is certainly slimmer. Image number four was taken in another prison yard, which must be either in Luneburg (where she was tried) or at Hamlyn (where she was executed). In this shot she is standing beside another female prisoner. She is wearing the same clothes, including the jackboots that were one of her trademarks of violence. She wore these in the Celle yard image, but now she is slimmer and looks far more composed. Photograph five is an image from her trial, taken by a court photographer. She is sitting in a row with other accused but has been distracted by something above her.

Like in all of the trial photographs, it's clear she has taken care with her appearance: she looks extremely calm, even demure, and aware of the camera. It is almost as if her mind is somewhere else. Number six is another courtroom shot, which may have been taken on the same day. In this image, again, something has caught her eye. Her demeanour has changed; contempt, or even anger, flickers across her face. This is the only image I have seen that hints at the character that hides behind appearances.

The unnerving thing about the first and last two images is not just her beauty but the fact that there is not a glimmer of the being that she was. Remembering the days when I spent so much time trying to read the appearance of people walking down the street, I realised that the image, even when it appears to be revelatory, is still a surface. Insofar as she perfected hiding everything about herself within her image, she became nothing but an image. The image bore no resemblance to the nature of the being it appeared to represent.

Overall, what I am left with, after looking at these six images and living with them for almost a lifetime, is that they are not only a facade covering something hideous but a message of absolute detachment. What her look says is that she is always elsewhere, never where she appears to be. In contrast to the other images of female guards I have seen, hers are remarkable. The history of the other women is present, existentially exposed by the marks of experience inscribed on their faces – the harshness of their actions has removed all sensitivity and coarsened their features; they look vacant. They are alive but their souls and humanity have departed. My mother was the exception. As I have been saying, she showed not a single sign of being destroyed by her acts of destruction.

For me, setting her history alongside her appearance produced something strange and unnerving. It went beyond the misfit between knowledge and image, her projected self and her actions. There was something present, but unseen, that she unwittingly managed to manufacture and express in her visual presence. For genetic reasons we looked almost the same, but my appearance had no relation to her being. I saw nothing of her in myself. We appeared to look the same but were fundamentally different. I told myself this a million times. Yet in my own way I was just as unreadable – my appearance also concealed rather than revealed. Eventually I realised that she was possessed, but not in the way this condition has traditionally been presented. Yes, there was something extremely malevolent present within her, but she was also possessed by a fantasy of herself; she perceived her appearance as modern and cinematic. In part I gained this understanding from a female Jewish doctor, a friend of the prisoner who was my mother's dressmaker. The doctor reported the dressmaker's observation of my mother sitting transfixed in front of a mirror. She often did this for hours on end; her eyes locked onto her own reflection.

Unquestionably she was narcissistically obsessed with her own image, so even while on trial for her life, as I have said, she groomed herself for appearance. The most important feature of the event for her was not those who judged her, but the presence of the camera.

This obsession had a demonic side and perhaps explains why she was driven to destroy the looks and related self-image of so many camp inmates. By disfiguring their faces and slashing their breasts she was making herself *the* singular figure of beauty. As one of the women who survived Auschwitz wrote: "She preferred hitting the faces of good-looking female prisoners with a whip." This survivor went on to say that one day she saw her "put out the eyes of a girl because she saw her talking with an acquaintance through the fence." As said, my mother's relation to beauty was to be its singular representative. There could only be one – her. In this respect, was beauty the essence of her madness, her evil? Was it her demon? I don't think it's hard to understand why I was always frightened when looking at images of my mother. They were indivisible from seeing myself. I emotionally recoiled from what I saw yet was equally and helplessly drawn to the six years of her short image-life that her photographs put before me.

As for narcissism, that's more complex, and was among the many questions that I still am unable to adequately answer. Notwithstanding that it was to become a directive force that indirectly shaped my life. The most commanding images of my mother were those where a gaze was directed at the viewer, seemingly with an invitation to look and admire, but which were really just for her own consumption. The image, the demeanour, the attention paid to her clothes were props and players in the fantasy she, centre stage, was acting out. The problem was trying to gain any sense of a script.

So often my search for knowledge was destined to end in disappointment. No matter what I studied or learnt, besides the negatives of a possible inheritance, evil and madness, I still did not *know* my mother beyond what she appeared to be. Eventually I came to realise that no matter what I learnt, it would never deliver decisive knowledge. Moreover, regardless of how well-informed I became, I knew the irrationality of my fundamental fears would remain. Thus, I never fully escaped wondering if and when my life would take a turn at some unexpected moment and deliver what I most feared. In particular, for a few years as a student, having some knowledge of mental illness, I was especially aware and worried about the fact that schizophrenia frequently arrived in young people in their late teens or early twenties. More than this, I wondered, if it happened, would I be able to recognise what was occurring before it was too late?

What was especially reinforced during my postgraduate career was that, in some way or another, concerns about the past, my mother and myself were going to be more than forceful direct influences on my life: they were going to be its essence. I was already aware that these concerns substantially affected my interpersonal relationships and the nature of my study interests. Finally, I realised that I was dealing with something that was not just about me.

To deal with the final destination in the enactment of my mother's depravity I need to say something about Bergen-Belsen. Reading about the horrors of this camp is gut-wrenching for anyone. However, the documented accounts of the liberation are sanitised. It was hard reading a wide range of accounts in the knowledge that one of the most brutal and depraved female camp guards was my mother. This was the situation wherein I was conceived and from which I emerged, and reading about the place and watching documentary films about the camp, made me vomit many times. Sometimes my eyes were sore from crying and many sleepless nights. While I looked and felt ill, I could not stop: I had to know.

To comprehend just how appalling Bergen-Belsen was, it is necessary to know a little of its history and character as a wasteland of humanity wherein the bounds of suffering were reached and exceeded. It was established in March 1943. Initially it was meant to be a camp for prominent Jews who could be exchanged for Germans interned in other countries. But by 1944 it had been reassigned as a "recovery camp" for prisoners who were too weak to work (their real designation being "unproductive"). No additional medical facilities were added to support this function. In effect, it was a place to send the sick and starving to die rather than to recover. By the end of 1944 there were more than 15,000 inmates. Within four months this had risen to more than 41,000, of whom 18,000 died within a month. As the Germans retreated, they relocated prisoners to Bergen-Belsen from Auschwitz. These people came without food or water, with many of them suffering from typhus. Just before this process started, my mother gained a transfer to the camp to join her boyfriend. The place quickly became a literal nightmare. Typhus raged, and my father was one of its victims. For fear of contagion, the guards withdrew and left the *Kapos* to keep order.

By the first week of April, the camp, which was a conglomerate of five camps (one of which was a special facility to house "habitual criminals, felons and homosexuals," with others for Hungarians, women, non-German Jews plus general mixed groups) had a combined population of over 60,000.

On April 15, 1945, troops from the British 7th Armoured Division arrived in the area, and on April 17 the camp was liberated. What these troops found was described in the press as an actual "hell on earth." The camp was a mass of the dead, dying, disease and excrement. The sight and the stench were indescribable. It was estimated that around 28,000 people died in the period immediately after liberation. The camp was locked down because of typhoid and typhus. Prior to liberation, there was no food or water for six days and chaos reigned, with the living clamouring for the sustenance they needed to survive. Accounts of this period are more than harrowing. Many were killed (not least by club-wielding *Kapos* on the rampage). More died because they were unable to digest the food provided to save their lives. The place was littered with piles of bodies. After liberation, as a punishment, camp guards were forced, without gloves or masks, to bury tens of thousands of bodies. As they moved the bodies, limbs often came off in their hands.

Dante could not have imagined anything that exceeded the depth of inhumanity that Bergen-Belsen manifested. Its horror and suffering were beyond the reach of language and image. Yet this is the place and moment into which I was born. How could coupling, conception and coming into the world in such a place not mark my soul?

To help deal with the situation the British turned an adjacent barracks into a hospital staffed by the Royal Army Medical Corp. This was the hospital where I was born. Rehabilitating the former prisoners was a slow process, as was finding somewhere willing to accept them. It took five years to close Bergen-Belsen, and then it was razed by fire in September 1950. Bergen-Belsen is twenty-four kilometres from Celle. I know the prison where my mother was first held – it's not far from my home. I know why in sorrow, not guilt, I have to end my days here. The fact that I cannot forget my mother is my problem. But making unforgettable the conditions that enable people like her to exercise power and act must concern all thinking people, as is the need for a level of understanding that recognises the inadequacy of evoking the concepts of evil and madness as if they carried consensual meaning.

8

The Trial

I tried to assess the veracity of all the voices that have spoken of my mother by cross-referencing them. Besides historical documents, including those created in the course of her trial and its subsequent reports, there were many newspaper and magazine articles, scholarly papers, books and plays about her. I think I have read them all, some many times. Different portrayals of my mother have been created, many of them contradictory.

For my part, I was looking for signs that prefigured *me*. My search was for anything that appeared to match with my traits beyond our similar appearance. What I did now seems crazy. For instance, I analysed her trial transcripts to see if I could discover non-linguistic and linguistic sound patterns and inflections of speech that I displayed when I wrote or spoke German. I can't believe how stupid and irrational I was in doing this. She was an uneducated German peasant, while I was highly educated and my dominant language was English. What a fool's errand.

What I should have realised was that my father was educated, and much smarter than my mother. If there was evidence to be found, which was not the case, there may have been a remote possibility that my intellect owed something to him and his mental characteristics. Despite my efforts I know almost nothing about him besides his age, what I can see from a blurred single photograph of him and the basic information that he was in the SS, an engineer of some kind, transferred from Auschwitz to Bergen-Belsen. He died of typhus just before the camp was liberated.

As I have repeatedly expressed, fear has been a driving force of my life. The mist of fear fell over everything I saw and thought, even while I was excelling in academia. I also have to say that increasingly I lived with another emotion that insinuated itself into my life: a deep, deep, sense of sadness.

I bring these remarks to my reading and reaction to the transcripts of interviews with people who were witnesses for the prosecution and defence at her trial, the remarks of judges and the trial reports in the press. It was this material that gave me the clearest sense of just how much truth was revealed and the extent to which it was tampered with. While I have said my mother was not smart it was obvious that she was cunning. I also realised that although the evidence against her was extensive and damning, it was only part of a much larger, unreachable picture.

The trial was equally opaque. Certainly, there were issues of inadmissible evidence, but above all I understood that the most damning evidence against her rested with those who could not speak: the dead. I also knew her words were strategic – she was intelligent enough to know that she couldn't pretend to be innocent and, to be credible, had to admit a degree of guilt. To tell the whole truth would have been totally self-damning. Whatever she said, she was trying to save her life. There was, however, one moment of unambiguous truth. It was when Helen gave character evidence and told the story of her sister's expulsion on the day her father thrashed her and threw her out because she arrived in the uniform of a SS *Aufseherin*. As will be remembered, she never returned to her family home again. The point to be made came from the media reports of Helen's account. When the story was told, my mother sobbed uncontrollably. This was the only reference to an overt expression of emotion that I discovered. It partly reframed the questionable authorship of the letter to her father and affirmed her emotional input into its content, if not her actually writing words on the page.

Encountering the actual treatment of my mother by the media was one of the most unpleasant experiences. They took advantage of her youth, beauty and brutality to sensationalise what she was. There were headlines like "Beautiful Beast," "Killer Bitch" and "Nazi She-Devil."

Facing the facts of her adult life was truly awful, but in a way, the comic-book fiction created over the years by the media (as it authored the popular memory of her) was even worse. In contrast, I read books and the script of a play based on her adult life, which were more serious and measured. What begs emphasis here is that while she may well have been evil, bad and mad, the makers of her hyper-sexual, sensationalised, sadomasochistic image did a disservice to women more generally. The media used the fantasy she constructed of herself to author an even more extreme and insidious sexist stereotype of the Nazi jack-booted woman, whip in hand, foot on the back of the neck of a naked, willing victim gaining pleasure from sexual degradation. Seeing this imagery and knowing the real consequences of her depravity gave me a feeling of nausea.

The fact, as I have said, that there is so little known about her life made it all the easier to present her via a fictional one-dimensional horror story mostly divorced from facts. A significant problem resulting from this representation was the gross disrespect it showed toward her victims.

I have two particularly nasty stories that I need to tell. The first was a short account of her hanging that appeared in *Readers Digest* in the late 1950s, authored by her executioner: I will say something about him later. The article mysteriously arrived anonymously in the post a few days before Christmas in 1976. The pages had been roughly torn out and stuffed into an envelope. The handwritten envelope (which I kept along with the article) was sent by airmail from London. Why, at this moment, by whom, and by what means had they gained knowledge of me and my address? I still have no idea. Aunt Helen was the only person who knew who my mother was – in some way, by intent or error, she had to be connected.

More recently, I discovered a stream of sickening and stupid rubbish on the Internet by members of her neo-fascist fan club in Europe and the US. Again, I will come back to this later, but for the moment a question arose: Did this material affect how I viewed and thought about my mother?

The answer is yes, but not dramatically. But at the same time there were surprises that made me reflect on the material I have read and reread. I found that I positioned my mother with more nuance. I gained a greater sense of how, within Nazi culture, psychological research showed that a small percentage of people ran out of control. SS training took "normal" people and produced cruel and unfeeling men and women. It did not create sadists and sexual perverts, yet it effectively put people who were actual or latent sadists and sexual perverts in a situation that gave them both the opportunity and licence to act without constraint. I also gained a clearer grasp of my mother's narcissism, and, above all, of a life damaged beyond comprehension or redemption.

I asked myself: What if she had become a nurse? Would all that lurked within her been repressed? Could she actually have become a caring person? As a nurse, would she have been one of the many Nazis whose beliefs washed away in the tide that surged over a regime now globally viewed as despicable in the decades after the fall of the Third Reich? I reminded myself that she proclaimed her allegiance to "the cause" to the very end, including her assertion in her letter to Helen: "I am dying for my country." From the moment of her unrestrained attraction to the Hitler Youth League of German Girls she was wedded to the Nazi cause.

My mother's cunning became more visible during her trial. Historically, she constructed different images of herself for different audiences. Camp inmates experienced her as a vicious *Aufseherin*. For those who tried her, she acknowledged her violence toward prisoners, but restricted it to its milder forms as if they were acceptable. To Helen she presented herself as innocent, at a meeting they had after she left Auschwitz in 1945, but before she moved to Bergen-Belsen. At that meeting she lied and told Helen that she worked in the post office sorting mail and from time-to-time was detailed to do guard duties. As I realised long after our parting Helen never got over the discovery of what her sister had become. I now feel sure this is why she tried to erase her memories of the past.

While I read the trial transcripts, I looked again at the photographs that were taken at the time to see how my mother presented herself (sensual, demure, aloof, annoyed). The images manifested her different personas, but they were at odds with her reported and confirmed camp behaviour, which was unreservedly malicious, aggressive, vindictive, violent and cruel. The only common factor in every context was her narcissism. There were many stories about this trait, and they etched an indelible, if invented, image in my mind – a composite image, constructed from reports presented at her trial, of a vain strutting woman, immaculately dressed in a finely tailored and pressed SS uniform, polished and gleaming jack boots, with a silver-plated pistol in the holster in her belt, and her famed horse whip of plaited cellophane in her hand. The unreality was a character in a movie set, but its actuality was in a concentration camp. She created a completely inflated sense of power by appearance. Apparently, she boasted both to other guards, and to prisoners, that after the war was over, she was going to become a movie star. Such a projected image – both fact and parody – is ridiculous and sad. It is the image she saw of herself when she looked in the mirror, or at photographs of herself.

Yet she lived this illusion in a bizarre way. It was acted out in her movie-set imaginary of everyday camp life. She adopted roles, and her *grotesque* actions had a performative dimension inviting the gaze of onlookers. She even treated the court, in which she was on trial for grave offences, as a stage on which to appear. I gained this view by assembling her courtroom press pictures and accounts of her conduct during the trial. It was clear that she worked hard to make herself a photogenic presence. The media fell for it. As I mentioned, her jacket and skirt were ironed daily, her hair was constantly toyed with and looked as if she had just stepped out of a fashionable hairdresser. This was in contrast to the women around her who looked downtrodden, sad and drab. Rather than pay attention to the events unfolding, she primarily paid attention to herself and to those looking at her. The most revealing example was when a film of the appalling conditions of Bergen-Belsen was shown and everyone in the courtroom, including the accused, showed signs of distress, except her. She looked around, examined her nails, adjusted her hair and seemed bored. Not the least vestige of empathy for people as human beings remained in her. Another memorable story came from the autobiography of a camp inmate, a Jewish doctor, who had a lot to say about my mother and her obsession with appearance. The doctor told of camp inmates lining up to go to their deaths after the gas chamber selection process. She commented, with incredulity, that some were captivated by my mother's beauty, and a few were heard to comment on it. Certainly, the trial press photographers couldn't keep their cameras off her. Every day she was photographed arriving, sitting in the courtroom playing to the cameras, and departing. She was an "evil demon of the image" with magnetic power.

Finally, there are two stunning remarks associated with the aftermath of her trial. They come from her executioner. The man hanged around a hundred war criminals, but my mother was the first woman. In press reports at the time he recalled the moment when, accompanied by guards, she approached the gallows. As he wrote later: "She came walking towards me laughing and she seemed as bonny a girl as you would wish to meet. It was a hard job, and it shook me up." Reports said that after the executioner hanged her and two other women, he was visibly shaken.

A few years later, after he retired, he wrote about this moment at length in the *Reader's Digest* article anonymously sent to me. It's worth quoting in full:

> When she came towards me laughing and smiling, I froze. This was my first lass to drop since taking up the job as a hangman. I had topped a good few that deserved to drop, but nobody before or after ever smiled at me. It took me a moment or two to recover. Then thoughts came to me from all directions. I had to make a

special effort to stay calm and remain expressionless. Her smile faded in my mind, but not totally. I put all thoughts of her aside and quickly did what I had to do. She shouted "*schnell,*" and then kissed the bible the priest held out for her to touch. I then put the hood over her head, the rope around her neck, and said what I always say under my breath "please God forgive me" and hit the trap release. Afterwards I just looked at her for the full two minutes as she hung there lifeless, her neck broken. I then lowered her and the body was put in a coffin. The press were right: she was beautiful. I couldn't reconcile what I saw with what I knew. What really perplexed me was that friendly almost alluring smile. Why? How could she do that at this moment of finality? Why so relaxed. It was extraordinary. I knew I had hung the right person. I knew she was really bad, but it didn't feel like it. She was so young, and so bonny. I can still see that smile.

So even at her very last appearance she gave a performance. After her execution, along with ten others, she was buried in the courtyard of Hamlyn Prison. A few years later the bodies were moved to a wood a few kilometres away. This was because, as the last obscenity, the Hamlyn grave became a shrine and a place of pilgrimage for neo-Nazis. They turned her into an icon of German fascist womanhood, presenting her as a courageous and heroic figure whose life should be honoured and celebrated. In their twisted narrative she was made a scapegoat. Not only do neo-Nazis keep the lie alive but they spread it with the help of the Internet.

I could never visit her grave. Such a proximity, even in death, was beyond me. But I did eventually visit my birthplace, Bergen-Belsen. People talk of belonging somewhere. That hateful place is where I belong, not because of any attachment, but because it was where I was born and the only place where I was actually physically close to my mother. It was my place of origin, a fact I realised from which I could no escape. Somehow it was this that brought me to Celle, and completed by journey. I can't explain, it just felt right.

9

Impossible Relationships

While my mother spent a lot of time in front of a mirror looking at herself, she did so without in any real sense being able to see who and what she was. In contrast I spent a good deal of my life obsessively looking at her image and deeds as they appeared to me, and to others, knowing a good deal about what she was, but ever concerned about the retention of my sanity.

I became acutely aware of how contradictory my psychoneurotic condition was, having for such a long time existed in a state of constant terror about what I might be, knowing that the only way I could deal with it was to confront this condition. In this way I objectified myself for myself, not as if I were a doctor identifying symptoms and specifying a course of treatment but rather as an auto-analyst talking myself into a cure, or at least, a condition of coping.

Over time, I developed a conversation with myself about the distress in which I lived. What I came to realise was that there was no distinction between my distress and the distress of the human condition itself, of which the Holocaust was, and is, viewed as an extreme and overt marker. It was the distress of the German condition. My inner voice was an echo of the repressed though sometimes uttered voice of a nation confronting, refusing, acknowledging, all at the same time, a history of its captivation by the seductive power of evil and its image. A nation awaiting the death of the generation of the guilty. My silence was its silence. This was not the silence of the guilty, but another kind: the silence of shame. This shame, as Primo Levi put it, is about the "unspeakable flaw in all of 'us' which ever persists" and is evidenced by the unbroken history of genocide that ever folds back into silence.

Placed in this context, it was the extremity of my situation that made a self-confrontation unavoidable. For the vast majority of people, the distress of the discovery of the continual inhumanity of humanity is concealed under layers of fabrications of assigned "not me" otherness, and "civilisation." Yet the horror always returns in the same way, as an event of shame and media outrage, that mostly fades after a few days, its memory swept aside by the next topic of concern. Not only was the Holocaust an extreme example of such a force of negation but also of forgetting to confront "the flaw" it carried. As has been pointed out by numerous thinkers, there never was anything, as subsequent history confirms, to prevent the return of such abominations. Horror recedes into our collective past, and undoubtedly travels into our future. The dominance of the propensity of cultures to forget what is essential to remember means that the same danger is eternally destined to return. It is true that a minority do have a degree of awareness, but lacking any sense of agency to be able change anything, they turn away. Few have touched the dark side of the beings that we are, but life for them thereafter is unavoidably lived in the perpetual pain of this knowledge. Nonetheless life asserts itself: it goes on.

In the midst of my distress, I resolved I had to change my relationship with myself, and the few others to whom I had proximity, notwithstanding my fears about the unwelcome arrival of the cursed touch gifted by my mother. I knew my fears were irrational, but knew equally that they could not be erased by reason. Importantly, I came to realise that what I was living with was not what I feared but rather fear itself: in many ways fear made me and asserted what I am.

With this qualification, I want to say something about the fear and my belated acceptance that I am not my mother's daughter. I can't deny the biological link, but I have not been inducted into the relation of mother and daughter. The relationship I had with my aunt was never its surrogate. While I called her mother, I now realise it was a word without meaning or emotional significance.

As I got older, I traded on my seeming history of normality to tame the sense of panic that my fear induced. Nonetheless I continued to fret over the possibility of finding myself in an unforeseen event that would trigger a move from the neurosis I knew I had, to some kind of psychotic act.

What I have just recounted was not the whole picture. The more I found out about my mother and her sexual deviation and narcissism, the more my fear acquired another dimension. Was I a pervert waiting to happen? While I never thought this to be so, in contradiction I developed an automatic recoil from feeling anything sexual about anybody, fearing I might have latent uncontrollable desires waiting to be triggered. Unfortunately, this went too far, to the point that for a year or so all feelings were driven underground – I felt nothing. I just became a brain. As I said earlier, I never went past superficial relationships. Yes, I did establish a few friendships but there was always a barrier that was never breached. I never told anyone about my mother, with the exception of a few shrinks I went to see when I was in my twenties. They were no help. Eventually I realised I was carrying a load that was impossible to put down. Freedom for me was to learn how to travel with the burden.

Maybe I give the impression that I carried all of this distress stoically, and if so, I need to correct this impression. At times I dipped deep into a bottomless well of unhappiness, at others into the boredom of myself with myself. Although I decided from an early age that I would never get really close to another human being, get married or have children, sometimes I was felled by the pain of the emptiness this brought. I just folded into a heap of grief for the never-to-be, and I mourned the absence of what I never had or would have.

But I did make a life for myself. I had a home I like, career I took pride in, work that I believed contributed to knowledge, a good rewards relation with many students over decades, a few valued friends, those cultural pleases that sustained me, especially the music that I loved, travel and keeping physically active. For most people my dominantly solitary would not seem to be desirable, but I do not feel lonely or lacking. It this is my chosen life and above all I am affirmative about having changed my relations to myself. While some of the old fears faded, new and different ones arrived, reinforcing the disabling consequences of my secret life. The more success I gained, the more I feared that an exposure of my history would destroy it. If this happened, I knew I would be unable to bear the prospect of pity or scorn: they were both the same. The very thought of being linked to my mother, and of being asked to talk about her, especially by popular media interviewers, was paralysing. This possibility was made even worse because I looked so much like her, and images of her were easy to find. I imagined seeing a picture of us side-by-side in a newspaper, magazine or on TV. I remember once, after a shower, writing on a steamed-up mirror in the bathroom, "The daughter is a look-alike of the beauty who was the beast."

It was out of this history of thinking about fear that I discovered it to be plastic. It could be moulded and could change shape. I no longer feared I might run amok with a meat axe in a shopping mall, but rather that I would destroy myself in the belief that I was already destroyed. Yet this fear passed. While it didn't go away the courage to confront it, to confront myself, gave me the strength to realise and value myself as I was.

Beyond this shift in awareness, three things kept me sane: music, gardening and walking. The latter I did every day, summer or winter, rain or shine. During the week I walked in my local park, and at the weekend I drove out of town. I enjoyed the pure life of every bird and animal I saw. I enjoyed the silent company of trees, their changing moods and anchoredness. Walking kept me in touch with my physical self, my animality. The briskness of my daily walk, the climbing of my usual hill, my level of endurance on a weekend hike provided something valuable beyond measure. I found it impossible to stay indoors all day. I always had to have a garden and time to tend it. It didn't matter how modest it was, it had to be kept tidy, pretty and productive. My priority was a good supply of herbs, salad and other vegetables. I really enjoyed these simple pleasures.

Emotionally, it was music that provided a release of my pent-up anxiety and unhappiness. It was music that restored me as myself and gave me joy. My dominant taste was melancholic; its sadness soaked up mine, and conversely, music that expressed pleasure allowed pleasure to reach me. Beyond its therapeutic use and value, music was pure emotional communication. It partly filled the lack of intimacy in my life.

Certainly, I had a few almost close friendships that mattered, and a number of others that were transitory. I did not exist in a total emotional desert, but the fact is that I am fundamentally alone, and will ever be so. I believe a dispassionate perspective of my history would suggest that I never had an adequate ability or idea of how to become a fully functional social being. Having a lot to hide, how could I possibly explain to someone else what I was unable to explain to myself? To even talk about having "problems" was unacceptable to me. That was boring. I felt the same way when I talked to shrinks. The prospect of being tolerated or viewed with pity horrifies me.

 General and eternal questions about evil and madness still arose. These two issues were permanent fixtures in the process of my thinking about her and myself. They shifted from being exclusively linked to a study about her to become a wider concern and a focus of independent critical inquiry. As such, they occupied a good deal of my academic life. To make sense of this, I need to spend time outlining my more mature thinking on my relationship with my mother. It had three perspectives.

The first went to the question of how my relationship to her was defined, be it hatred, loathing, contempt, pity, anger or whatever. The key factor here was, *who was I trying to define my non-relationship with*? Put another way: who exactly was that person I called my mother? All I really knew about her was representations and facts; I did not *actually* know her. Was she anything more than the sum of mostly negative information and limited and one-dimensional representations? Even if the whole person was bad, mad and unredeemable I still had a very limited picture. Consequentially I tried to go beyond acknowledging the areas of her life where information existed, and what I did was extremely circumscribed. For example, beyond the few fragments of information I had in relation to my father, I started to see him as a probe into the fantasy of her life. It was pointless to speculate on whether or not her relationship with him was more than purely sexual, or if it involved any deep affection. But how, I asked myself, did he deal with the horrors of her actions, which I'm sure he was aware of? There was something more to think about, if not know.

Then there was the issue of how the present always recasts one's views of the past. To take two obvious examples: at the end of World War Two the Holocaust was regarded as a catastrophe that blighted humanity and was never to be repeated. But in many respects, it has been repeated many times, through genocide and the denigration of human beings, and by people acting inhumanely *en masse* in Asia, Africa and Europe. These recent events not only recast how the past is seen and judged but also reconfirm the inhumanity intrinsic to humanity itself.

Another example goes to the relation of women to war, which has dramatically changed over the last seventy years or so. In the past women, at least in Europe, were not associated with military violence even though they served in the armed forces in support roles. There were a few exceptions, such as females in resistance movements. The women of the Waffen SS appeared as extreme and violent deviations from this history. Now, however, violence, killing and atrocity are not gendered. I recall the words of a female US Army senior officer in an article a while ago: "War is no longer a hormonal affair."

My biological bond connected me to *who and what* my mother was *and did*. I was in her womb when she committed atrocities; I was present: without choice, knowledge or sense, and this made me feel I was *organically* implicated. I felt like I was a bird in an egg, and one of those few birds that learn to sing before they hatch. No matter that I was completely innocent, unknowingly I was there, so something reached me. I had a debt I could not quantify, would never be able to pay but had to acknowledge.

There is a postscript on my father. From what I could find out, which was not much, I think he was likely to have been her first "normal" mature sexual partner. On first consideration I did not believe this could be correct. I thought it was another fantasy. But there are a few fragments of evidence that contradict this view. These come from recorded comments made by my mother during her trial: "Hatzie (what she called him) knows I'm telling the truth"; or the even weirder "I wish Hatzie could see me now." Of course, if my father had been present to witness her staged appearance he would also have been on trial. However, as I have said, he died of typhus. Her griefless comments were no doubt about a desire for admiration from him. She viewed him as her intimate admirer.

10

The Study of Evil

The study of evil has been a major part of my intellectual life and my lifelong preoccupation. Having said this, I need to reiterate that the meaning of evil is neither self-evident, clear nor fixed. While it is often treated as if it was obvious, the concept is actually elusive, subject to historical change and variably understood across cultures. As my knowledge about it changed, so my own understanding has been in flux. As I have said in many ways, I believed I was born out of evil environmentally and biologically. For a long time, it seemed as if evil had an amorphous materiality, which enveloped all that it was directed toward like a mist, gas or ether. Seen in relation to my mother, evil appeared to be an intrinsic quality of her being, a force she served as well as an animating characteristic of the environment of the camps in which she fully realised herself. Serving her masters in Auschwitz was indivisible from servicing the all-consuming fires of the camp's crematoria, which soon came to represent the fires of hell on earth.

Such was my mother's devotion to those causes and actions deemed evil, which constituted the very core of Nazism, that she went to her death proud of having served them. My father is a more ambiguous figure: yes, he was a member of the SS and, as an engineer, he was a camp functionary. There is no record of him having involvement in any atrocities in the company of my mother or anyone else. I'm sure, as an educated man and an engineer, he was smarter than her. I held onto this view as a glimmer of light in a well of darkness.

As an engineer, my father, although intelligent and educated, was an example of a flawed child of reason, like all thinking Nazis. I suspect his responsibilities were mostly in relation to overseeing small-scale construction works. The little additional information I gleaned from military records confirmed that he was born in Hildesheim on July 9, 1909. But I found no record of his birth in the register of births, deaths and marriages of the city. These records also showed that he joined the Nazi party on August 12, 1938, and then four months later the Waffen SS, which listed his civilian occupation as clerk, whereas the Bergen-Belsen records listed him as an engineer. I do not believe his military name was his real name. This is because I found no evidence of family, qualifications or where he was from. At this point I drew blanks. But I knew was that there was something mysterious about him.

While my mother was beyond redemption, and knowing him to be badly flawed, I thought that perhaps he still represented a source of my potentiality. He gave me a speck of hope. Nonetheless, and notwithstanding the presence of this hope, I know that if I actually discovered the existence of evil in some unambiguous form within me, I would have ended my life. I never viewed this prospect as an act of suicide, but rather as duty. No matter how irrational this view may sound to someone else, it made sense to me.

Effectively the more I knew about evil the wider the gap became between what I feared and how I actually experienced myself, and the more it became a central intellectual concern. Existentially I learned – but more importantly experienced – a very simple lesson: knowledge changed me. As a result, I came to realise that I was not just born into the evil of the Holocaust but into the shattering presence and agency of the plurality of evil as a latent and intrinsic quality of humanity itself. In fact, there was a *thetical* – that is, absolute – perceptual change in how I viewed the human psyche.

I have quite a lot to say about evil because my changing relation to it marked my life and what I am. But more than this, a particular understanding of evil insinuated itself into many cultures of the modern age as they tried to make sense of the Holocaust, as it layered onto the memory of World War One – that evil is a carnival of death and inhumanity runs out of control. Under these circumstances, it is as if something takes possession of military leaders that makes them incapable of halting the wanton sacrifice of life that their orders initiated. War is accepted as one of the ways that power functions geopolitically in the world. The claims to "just cause" for war in no way displace the raw fact that war is evil materialised. It is mass dehumanisation. It not only maims and destroys bodies, minds and spirits, but also has an aftermath of lifetimes. In war so many people lose who they are. They become something else, over which they have little control, and consequently they do monstrous things. My mother does not fold into this context: she was not under threat; she was not propelled by the heat and dynamism of battle. In her role as a camp guard, she did not exercise little control but rather no control.

I struggle to say what I aim to say without slipping into my academic persona. It's hard, because the language of evil is so exhausted and clichéd and so replete with banalities. I have to cut through it. I do not want to be heard as saying more of the same. I am well aware that for young people the events I'm talking about are far removed from the worlds they know, and that events I talk about exist as history and the stuff of movies. Yes, terrible things happen, but the Holocaust was something else. It was a terminal punctuation in Western modernity that foreclosed the West's illusory claim to being the culmination of modern civilisation. The horror it was, and manifested, failed to be grasped in the company of the genocidal and ethnocidal history of Western colonialism.

Over many centuries colonised people were subjugated, tortured and killed by warfare, abuse and being deliberately exposed to introduced diseases. In the Americas between 1492 and 1600, fifty-six million native people died. In India in from 1880 to 1920, a mere forty years, over one hundred million people died. Who knows the total number of perished, or how accurate estimates are, but what is beyond dispute is that the numbers are vast. The full implications of the violence and suffering of colonialism has still, in so many ways, not been grasped in the West. This history does not diminish the horror of the Holocaust but rather puts it into an unbroken continuum with the present.

What is so everlastingly shocking is that while the Holocaust occurred in Germany, a nation, as stated previously, that laid claim to be at the core of the creation of the Enlightenment, and thus the harbinger of Western humanism, its colonising dark underside went unnoticed. The chilling truth is that what was incinerated in the ovens of Auschwitz was not just bodies of Jews and others in the heartland of the West via industrialised means, but the global reality of the idea that humanity had progressed from savagery to a civilised condition. The Holocaust exposed this claim as being completely illusory. For all the trappings of a modern world and its culture, Homo sapiens, as Friedrich Nietzsche asserted, "ever remains the same." Amazing technology has been created, the world around us changes, sometimes for the better, often for the worst. Meanwhile we moderns, for all our sophistication and cultured surroundings, are fundamentally as flawed as we ever were. As the most dangerous of animals, we actually live an act of self-deception, a condition that can so easily be taken away. Our humanity hangs on a thread. It can easily be cut by a malevolent force, as fascism shows, and what then awaits is called evil.

Viewed against this backdrop I, like other people I know, despair at the ineffectuality and vacuous gesturalism of humanism. In saying this, it may seem as if I'm venting the frustration of one rational human being, but this is not so. Rather, what I'm really doing is attempting to put words to that scream of pain emanating from lives lived in proximity to ignorance that spawns war and the destruction of environments on which life depends. Ignorance that ignores the physical and mental violence of extreme poverty and oppression in which scores of human beings exist. My confrontation with this dark fact of life is unavoidable, but for the vast majority of people of privilege the reverse is true. They, their governments, the corporations and companies many of them work for, wilfully choose not to acknowledge the scale of human suffering, but equally that systemic injustice and inequity are a product of the afterlife of modernity.

It is important and sobering to add that not only is the irrationality of rational systems (as the organisational underpinning essence of the Holocaust demonstrated) alive and well, it is now larger and more vigorous than ever. Moreover, at some point, the nature of "the system" so understood is going to meet a political response to an unsustainable global population heading toward ten billion and a deep enviro-climatic and food crisis. The seeds of this mega-disaster can already be recognised in the ways refugees and the displaced are being detained in camps and detention centres that barely support life. All the indicators suggest that as numbers swell, the dangers coming from this situation are going to be massive and the conditions horrendous.

From my years of research, I concluded that the study of evil, situated as it was in the backwaters of theology and moral philosophy, was not treated as important. The imperative to create an adequate and contemporary understanding of it was not being fully grasped. Evil was left at rest, untroubled by interrogation. This alarmed me, especially now that destruction of life can be delivered in so many ways, and so quickly, by so many different technologies.

From what I have said it will come as no surprise that early in my postgraduate career I realised that evil was a neglected object of contemporary philosophical inquiry. It was clear that this unfashionable area of study needed to be made an object of public and academic concern – I found my mission.

Unsurprisingly, putting my history together with my study interests, I embraced the very things that deterred most others. I had to confront a large and pressing problem: what in the late modern age does evil mean at a fundamental level? I started asking this question in earnest as a postgraduate student at the end of the 1960s. Even though I ended up as a professor researching and teaching the philosophy of evil, I am still asking the same question.

As I have made clear, the question of evil has never just been an academic one, but rather one of life and death, freedom or oppression. But before going further I first need to backfill a few significant gaps about myself that I have passed over without comment.

After my first degree, fortune shone and I got a scholarship to undertake a doctorate in philosophy at the University of Berlin. Predictably my research was on the philosophy of evil. This gave me a chance to visit many places that marked my destiny – not least Ravensbrück and Auschwitz, but not Bergen-Belsen.

As ever I lived as a loner. I bypassed the tumult of student politics in the late 1960s and in my post-graduate years I stayed focussed. A few months after gaining my doctorate I gained a postdoctoral fellowship in the department of philosophy at Columbia University. I arrived in New York in 1972. I was 27 years old. By 1987 I was an associate professor of philosophy at the State University of New York, Stony Brook.

Starting as a high school senior, I spent 25 years studying and trying to understand evil. I taught courses on it, wrote papers and three books, and spoke at conferences. But while I had a great deal to say about how evil has been understood, I continually returned to my silent dialogue on how the question of evil shaped my view of my mother, and directed my life and, in many ways, my understanding of the modern world.

For me this whole enterprise was not, and still is not, an abstract academic exercise. Moreover, I came to the conclusion that understanding evil is more important than ever. Such understanding shows that it is actually complex, and far from self-evident. The challenge I have at this point of my story is again to explain this without falling further into the critical distance that is so easily created by an academic style of writing so familiar to me.

I am going to start by, again, pointing out that the concept of evil is still deployed in secular Western societies in the media, and in everyday life and popular culture, as if its meaning is self-evident. It still retains the same moral force that it had when societies were predominantly Christian. However, as I have said, the Holocaust shattered the authority of the theological foundations of the meaning of evil, which was founded upon two propositions. One was the notion of "moral evil" and asserted that evil is inherent in wicked actions, and their consequences are thus offences against God; as such they become sins. Proposition two asserts that evil is a feature of natural forces. In other words there is "natural evil" as evident in the suffering that humans and animals experience during and after the violence of natural disasters like earthquakes, droughts, and cyclones.

The whole theological discussion of evil, especially in religious philosophy, became deeply implicated in debates over the existence or non-existence of God. Without going into detail about these arguments, not least because they are not exactly entertaining, and getting out of them is not easy, I will point to a few things the philosopher Leibniz had to say about the concept of "theodicy" – a collection of ideas, criticisms and claims about the justice and goodness of God. Leibniz does this in the context of a widespread belief in the existence of evil in the world.

Gottfried Wilhelm Leibniz was one of the most significant Enlightenment philosophers. He was born in Leipzig in 1646, and was the son of a moral philosopher. While noted as a mathematician and philosopher of mind, what is of interest is that he rehearsed a series of arguments on the relationship between God, evil and the world. In these he put forward the view that God did not create a perfect world. By implication this meant that God did not choose the best course of action and lacked the power, knowledge or goodness to do so. The best course of action would have been to make a world without evil, and this would have been the "best of all possible worlds." The fact that this condition was not created was the proof that God did not exist. Another, and more succinct version of what Leibniz put forward was that if God existed there would be no evil, but there is evil, and therefore God does not exist.

Such thinking became grist to the mill of philosophy for centuries, and has been transposed to the view of the Holocaust, as an evil event which reaffirms that God does not exist. From this it follows that evil can no longer be designated as a failure of God, assigned to an absence of God, or asserted as a quality of the world, for it was demonstrably shown to have been manifestly created, and then delivered, by the application of an ideology that debased the humanity of one section of the human race by another that was more powerful. In a post-theological world, evil has no pre-existing presence in anything. It is simply the creation of human beings who were made evil by other human beings in infancy, childhood or adulthood.

Two-year-olds, for example, have been written about as monsters driven by unsocialised desires. Here, as evolutionary anthropology tells us, an infant is an animal *en route* to its humanness. Consider what would happen if this enfant had their cognitive and emotional development arrested from this moment onward, and then in their late teenage years they were released into the world. However they were viewed – as wild, mad, bad or evil – existentially they would be a product of how they were de-socially made, beyond conditioning and brainwashing. Now consider an adult placed in a violently dehumanising environment where there were only two ways out: kill or be killed. Some survive such an experience, others don't. They break. In this context one can ask, don't both examples show that evil acts cannot be judged by mere appearance, or reduced to the qualities of the brain of a malfunctioning being (which they might be), but need to be understood as something that is produced environmentally, socially, biophysically or psychologically? There are many "devils" that create evil. There are also forces that collectivise it and make it systemic. Whatever the cause, there is also doubt.

For all this we are still left with the question: what is evil? No matter the excessive cruelty and extended suffering of events like the Holocaust, it exceeds the violence of nature and the social relativism of wickedness. Such events – past and prospective – are without bounds, and they cannot be simply grounded in an aggressor and their victim, or in the act, the system, the moment and its afterlife, the abomination or its representation. They all defy language and knowledge. To observe evil is to see pleasure that delights in pain, without constraint, law, reflection or concern. But its essence still evades definition.

I wondered, could it be that the essence of both good and evil are beyond the reach of mind? Although claimed as manifest in the everyday they are also projected as being outside it. While Christian philosophical argument over good and evil continued after the Holocaust, it traded on consensual and ungrounded values that oscillate between contradictory and changing relations to right and wrong. Do not kill, do not lie, do not steal – but the government, church, capital and society do these things, and circumstantially justify their actions as moral. Evil appears before us constantly, nicely distanced by a screen as image or idea. Passively we watch. It is viewed as entertainment, even for children. Pleasure is taken in the horror of what is seen. Many times I have asked myself: is my fear of evil a liberated fear, a fear that is normality, the fear inherent in all of us?

After a lifetime of study, I struggle with the issue and with myself, and with the recognition that I still know little and understand even less. I could frame this with a philosophical diatribe, and trawl through a mountain of texts, mount a dualist critique of good and evil, as well as damn the Eurocentrism of such thinking. But in the end, I say what I have said, albeit in a more erudite way.

We retain a relation to "good" and "evil" as relativistic categories. What this means is that we think we know good and evil when we encounter them, but in so doing they are prefigured by the moral values that we have been inculcated into and have adopted. So, I can say my mother was an evil actor in an environment of evil on the basis not of a definition of evil but on the basis of my subjective interpretations of historical observations of evil in her reported actions.

These remarks don't assume, even with the qualifications made, that evil is obvious as absolute malevolence made visible, and so available to be collectively named. Rather it can hide in light as well as in darkness. It lies hidden, waiting for its moment to become active, directing a cast of agents and actors. This was certainly the case with German fascism, a regime for the most part enacted by ordinary people (a more frightening fact of evil's ordinariness than if they were evil mutant beings). The intent that was directive of so many evil actions in the camps came from elsewhere: a system of management (T4) and control that prompted, condoned and rewarded evil acts.

Perhaps there are a few saintly exceptions, but as the more perceptive commentators on people like my mother have pointed out, and as I have said, whatever these people's flaws, they are rendered unconstrained. They are made evil by the disposition of their flaws. One can again rightly extrapolate from this observation that the potential to become evil rests within us all to some degree. But most of us are not a product of environmental circumstances that predispose us to evil, often by exposure to coaching and the evil acts of others.

I remained uncertain about the depths of evil within me. I know how thin the veneer of humanness is, and how easily it can be fractured. Had my circumstances been less fortunate I might have broken. If I have given the impression that I have lived a pure and unblemished life, let me correct it: I have done bad things that I am ashamed of. But I don't think I crossed the line where rather than just hurting another human being I did them actual and irreparable harm. Having said this, one never knows. The damage we do to each other is so often hidden and its effects delayed until circumstances change.

As for my mother, I now have *some* understanding of what constituted her evil nature, but questions remain. I am still troubled by knowing that there is something uncanny about her. The strangeness can be read as sign of what possessed her, and can be seen in the smile that so unnerved the hangman.

11

Dialogues with the Living and the Dead

Besides the people I have already mentioned, during my career I had a number of good but not really close friends. There were two colleagues I socialised with, and then there was my next-door neighbour of more than thirty years. She was my gardening soul mate and more. Elizabeth and I walked together in the early morning several times a week for years, swapped novel and recipes, have coffee together at least twice a week, sometimes have breakfast at the Café Refugio Haus on Sundays, and occasionally go to concerts together. Most important of all, throughout my life I stayed friends with my musical school friend, Karen. I also had three students I took through from pups to PhDs who never quite left me – I'm not sure if they became my family or I theirs. And then there was Christopher.

He was a philosopher. Many years ago, I wrote to him to say how much I enjoyed the book he wrote on Nietzsche and music – notwithstanding the fact that jazz was my first love. Nietzsche declared that "life without music is error." That's exactly how I felt. Besides being a composer, Nietzsche's involvement with music extended to his fated friendship with Wagner. Nietzsche wrote about music in his short book, *The Case of Wagner* (written in 1888, which was shortly before his physical and mental collapse). In it, Wagner is identified with music of the damp North, in contrast to Bizet, whose work is characterised as belonging to the South, in its lightness and brightness. Anyway, as a result of my letter to Christopher, a dialogue began that lasted many years.

Like me, Christopher was damaged goods, in his case as a result of the Vietnam war. Shrapnel from a mortar shell took his physical manhood and more besides. We both acknowledged how our pasts had delimited and directed our future, but, once acknowledged, we never talked about them. What I know he mostly implied rather than ever explicitly stated. In this way we somehow communicated that we were both "orphans of a horror," and our inner suffering was our bond. No questions were ever asked. Our relationship was one of mutual understanding and total and uncritical acceptance. The friendship was special and meant a lot. I discovered I could leave a door in my life closed and locked and still have a relationship with another human being that was almost authentic.

When I first got to know him, Christopher was teaching at Northwestern University at Evanston, near Chicago, but within a year he moved to the University of Virginia, Charlottesville. We were now within easy striking distance of each other. Initially he drove to visit me every couple of months and we spent a weekend in New York to attend a concert or theatre production, have a good meal and coffee, do a lot of talking and always have a walk in Central Park. Then, before the start of the summer vacation in 1989, I had a call from Karen to say she was going on tour to Europe and would I like the use of her apartment for a month? I instantly said yes. It was a great place near Central Park, a few blocks west of the Whitney Museum. I knew it well and had stayed there maybe ten times, mostly for long weekends, and once for two weeks. She also used to visit me on Long Island, so we would see each other every few months. Besides having a great location and being a place of modest size, tastefully furnished, her apartment's great attraction was her music collection. It was mostly on vinyl, and you could lose yourself in it forever.

I was so pleased with the offer that I called Christopher to tell him the good news. He said he would love to come to New York for a week. We had a great time, and from that year on we had vacations together. One year we went to his folks' place in Vermont. They were warm and friendly people, who lived modestly above their small bookshop in Sherbrooke. Another year we spent two weeks in Hawaii, and went to San Francisco twice.

Somehow our conditions of sexual impossibility made friendship possible. We clicked intellectually and started writing papers together. We also planned a book, but it never happened. I felt like it would put too much weight on the situation we had created, and likely shift it out of balance. Above all we had wonderful and long running philosophical discussions. Christopher's main area of scholarship was nineteenth century French and German philosophy. We had robust and productive arguments; we learnt from each other. But in the end what united us was very simple, and had nothing to do with our intellectual lives. We were two people who recognised in each the depth of unhappiness and emotional pain we had experienced but who nonetheless made a positive and rewarding life against the odds. This silent spiritual kinship acted as the real foundation of our friendship. Although fated to be completely asexual, I didn't have a close relationship with another man. It sounds trite, but we were like brother and sister who were also friends. I think we were also something else, but it had no name. To look at us we could have been related: we were around the same height, age and complexion and were both slightly overweight, but the really strange thing was, we shared an ability to respond to each other verbally before the issue commented upon was even spoken. Yet in our closeness a certain distance remained.

I have more to say about Christopher later, but I want to say something about dead friends I never knew. These people are the key thinkers that I mentally lived with. They not only occupied my mind but, in many ways, created it. I didn't simply read these people but internalised their thoughts: they existed within me. We travelled on buses together, stayed up into the early hours. What I got to know was how to think with and like them. Having said this, for all the familiarity I gained with their thought, as people, they remained essentially unknowable. Even though I knew this, I still told myself that, somehow, I could sense something of their presence, something beyond my understanding of the words on the page. No doubt my fiction was not their fact, but nonetheless they were felt to be real companions.

For almost everyone outside of academic life the academic persona is off-putting; it alienates people. Worst of all is when it arrives as a conspicuous display of erudition. I say this because mention of the thinkers has nothing to do with the games that academics are so fond of playing. Rather, my relation to these thinkers, while based on engaging their ideas, was only directed at and connected to my inner life. They also had a discernible presence in how I presented myself to the world. What their thinking enabled me to do was get closer to my emergent understanding. Thus, I got a better sense not just of what I understood, but how. I say this without the expectation that it makes sense to anyone because it was a lived relation rather than an intellectual connection.

The insights I gained were from three people: two from the ancient world, Greece and China, and one from the modern.

The Greek is Euripides. He was the author of many tragedies, and what he had to say was relevant to my concerns. The most significant of his stories was that of Medea. The crux of this story is that when Medea's husband Jason (of Golden Fleece fame) abandoned her for another woman, she murdered her two children as an act of revenge, sacrifice, punishment. The issue, and the historical debate, that became the basis of my imagined conversation with Euripides, centred on the conflict between the emotions of love and revenge. Medea already had a history of murder – in order to escape her barbaric homeland, she killed her brother, cut his body into many pieces and "scattered them asunder." She did this to slow down her pursuers while making her escape with Jason. She also killed the King of Corinth and his daughters.

 History has presented Medea as a monstrous mother. She loved her children, but this love was overwhelmed by her desire for revenge, which at the moment of the terrible act was the more powerful of the two emotions. I compare Medea with my mother. As far as I know, there was no emotional conflict within my mother. After she gave birth, and left an instructional note on the blanket covering me, I didn't exist. So, my question to Euripides, in full knowledge of the mores of his age (which clearly did not match our own), was this: is there a crime a mother can commit against her children that is greater than murder?

My answer would be yes. If asked what this crime could possibly be I would name not an act of perversion or physical abuse but the negation of a child's existence. The murder of a child, or any act inflicted upon it, acknowledges its existence, but its negation does not. It is death before death.

Whereas my conversation with Euripides was terminal, the one created with Zhuang Zhou is ongoing. He lived in China around 2,300 years ago (while Euripides lived a hundred years or so prior). He is claimed by eminent Sinologists to be the author of a book whose title is translated as *On the Principles of Vital Nourishment*. The title of this work goes to a historically significant principle of Chinese life summed up in what was, in the nation's past, a well-known phrase still remembered by some: "to feed one's life."

Whereas many of my dialogues with the dead were about understanding, or coming to terms with the past, the one I had with Zhou always carried me to the future. It helped me live, gave me hope. I owe a debt of gratitude to Christopher, who introduced me to Zhuang Zhou.

Before going further, I should say what "vital nourishment" is. In essence, it relates to the feeding of everything that prolongs life in every respect. Therefore, it means feeding the body, the mind, the spirit and the soul. It also implies an active life of making and affirming life itself. This is in contrast to the pursuit of pleasure as the basis of happiness. Vital nourishment so understood is not a preoccupation with preserving one's own life but rather, the giving of life to life. It expresses a profound truth that many philosophers have uttered over the eons, namely, that to have a meaningful life, one's life has to be risked. One cannot hold onto life by clinging. Rather, it has to be given away to and by living. Living gives life to life.

There were two specific sentiments that powerfully asserted themselves, and they drove the central and constantly-repeated question in my dialogue with Zhou. The first was the importance of giving up our attachments to things because they blocked our being-in-process. What this means is putting oneself in a position of giving over to, and arrival in, emptiness and filling, the essence of change as loss and gain. Things so framed are anchors: they keep us where we are, and on multiple levels. The key term here is "giving up" – and the point at issue is attachment, not possession. The second sentiment had a profound and therapeutic impact, and it was an abandonment of the search for happiness.

Such a search presumes a lack to fill, and thus views one's life as framed by unhappiness. To have the one, the other has to exist, whereas the aim for Zhou was to disassociate from both and to occupy a nourished condition of acceptance of self. To abandon the search for happiness was to acquire freedom from eternal loss. This does not presume a painless "new age" condition of peace.

The last of the three on my list of influences is the philosopher Emmanuel Levinas, because of what he had to say about evil. Until his death in 1995 Levinas was a professor of philosophy at the Sorbonne in Paris and Director of the *École normale israélite orientale*. To understand why he is someone I would want to talk to I need to say a little about him.

Levinas was born in Lithuania in 1906. His parents were Jewish and he was inducted into Orthodox Judaism at an early age. This attachment profoundly influenced his life and his philosophy. By 1930 he was living in France, had become a French citizen and was establishing himself as a scholar. A decade later he was a prisoner of war. He was unluckily lucky. While serving as a French military officer he was captured by the Nazis. As a result, rather than finding himself in a concentration camp, he was sent to a prisoner of war camp. His camp number was 1492 (besides being the year the New World was "discovered," 1492 was also the year all Jews were expelled from Spain). As a member of a Jewish forced labour work group his life was hard, but he survived. His parents and brothers, who remained in Eastern Europe, were not so fortunate. Happily, his wife and daughter went into hiding in France and were safe. He was not the best-known French philosopher of his age, but he exerted a huge influence over other thinkers who gained higher profiles. Moreover, as time passed, his status grew.

I think it fair to say that as a religious man, philosopher and direct witness to the evil of fascism, he would have given his camp experience a lot of thought. Thus, what he had to say about evil is somewhat surprising. But before coming to this, what made him important for me was what he had to say on "the face." Thereafter we will come to his perspective on ethics.

The face occupied a major place in Levinas's thinking. Given the amount of time I spent looking at photographs of my mother, it is not hard to grasp why what he has to say on the face was of special interest.

One important observation made by Levinas is that we recognise who and what we are *in the face of an Other*. In silence, what we are is communicated to us. My mother was preoccupied with looking at her own face to create a mask. Evil was not visible there and remained hidden behind her deceptive beauty until that moment when her true horror was revealed to others. But not by her: she remained blind. All she saw was herself in her mirrored reflection. The Other was either rendered faceless, or went unseen and did not appear, or if chosen to be seen, was disfigured.

What Levinas said about the face changed how I looked at the pictures of my mother, others and myself. Importantly, Levinas tells us that the face cannot be possessed. It "resists" those powers that attempt to possess it. It is seen like a star in the immensity of space – what we see we cannot know, yet we try hard to do so. What we see is not the Other but our self. The face, in its epiphany, as an epiphany, is a reflection in which "I" see my "self." Which is to say that it displays a reaction to me by which I recognise myself. This does not mean that the communication is transparent – reaction cannot be taken to be a correspondence between cause and effect. Yet "the face speaks to me" and invites me into an incommensurate relationship. But whatever "expression" is seen, it does not arrive as a "true representation." The face is not true. I look at my mother's face: it is not true. Its beauty is a lie. Beneath it is something ugly, something destroyed, and questions that cannot be answered. As said before, I see my own visage, and it troubles me.

I now come to what Levinas thought about evil and why his insights on this subject became important. The central feature of his thinking is "excess," and the place evil plays in our lives as anxiety, which he called "the cutting point at the heart of evil." He believed that evil underscores the pain of life, which he understood as sickness, corruptibility, and perishability, that exists while we live and ensures that we die. Anxiety here is not a mild background concern generative of unease. Rather it is a major force, deemed to be the "root of all social miseries," derelictions, humiliations. Even more than this, anxiety and excess, in Levinas's presentation of evil, take us to the "end of [our] world." Rather than meaning that it delivers us into oblivion, Levinas meant that *evil ends our humanity*, it takes us out of ourselves, and so ends what we are. Now, perhaps, we can see that historically, including in the context of the Holocaust, things start to fall into place.

The manufacture of anxiety about the Other – the Jew, homosexual, criminal, nomad, communist – became a condition able to inflame and drive the excess of German Fascism. The anxiety created was used to feed a fear to be directed against that which was deemed to threaten. Evil thus exists outside reason, and is taken there by anxiety. Here is why reason is unable to define and describe the essence of evil. It is alien to reason in a way that unreason is not, for evil can occupy and employ both. As such we can also see its relation to excess – reason is excessively excessive in its power to corrupt and negate.

What comes next is going to be hard to deal with, but it cannot be otherwise. Excess is loss. It is without control. Excess is the underpinning of cruelty, greed, pain, and inhumanity. The camps were excessive. Their overwhelming material lack was created by that excessive designation of alterity that rendered the Other absolutely and totally abject. In other words, it was not just that other human beings were treated inhumanly, but that these beings were not fundamentally seen to be human, at least by the most cognitively colonised of their oppressors. This reduction is not new or absent in the present. It is intrinsic to the history of colonialism.

What Levinas pointed out, and which struck home so powerfully, was that evil cannot be accommodated into anything. It cannot be integrated. It was for him the "non-integratability of the non-integratable." Evil is foreign to everything.

In the fiction of my dialogue with Professor Levinas I ask him why his account of evil was apparently so oblique. The answer I feel he would have given is that, because of its excessiveness, it is not appropriate to locate evil in any particular time or event (including in his own history). So, in order to comprehend its true magnitude, one had to provide a way to understand that it was more comprehensive and overarching than any specific instance – the example cannot stand for the whole. While superficially it can seem that his account reads as abstract and perhaps obscure, the reverse is the case. In fact, with a little work, it disclosed a great deal, and this is what I have set out to show.

There is one last thing that Levinas gave me that has remained lodged in my mind and heart, and that is his critique of humanism, which he pointed out was simply not humane enough. And finally, from all my mental conversations with him, a paramount lesson I learnt is the cry: You carry in front of you the burden given you by your life. You travel toward it.

Of all the conversations I had with Christopher it was those about Levinas and evil that were the most fraught. In hindsight they portended problems ahead.

12
Conversations with the Psychos

In time, reason, knowledge and determination pushed the fear of my mother's presence out of the forefront of my mind, psyche and soul, but her shadow, and residual doubts about my connection with her remain and arrive uninvited – mostly in relation to the question of madness. Unlike evil, madness can be clinically described, and there are genetic connections to mental disorders. Also, I had history of being mentally ill. Thinking that madness might be my fate therefore did not seem to be an implausible prospect. I only mention it because it provides a contextual setting for the issues I am about to consider.

Considering yourself to be possibly mad, with the term "madness" being a catchall for all categories of mental illness, is almost like an invitation to become so. I remember a story Christopher told me about a soldier he knew in Vietnam who hated the army so much he decided to "work his ticket" (a British term meaning doing something that will result in being medically discharged for psychiatric reasons). This sane man played mad. He sat down every day in the dirt and made a mark in it with a stick, no matter what was done to him. Regardless of what he was meant to be doing he would disappear, later to be found, sitting in the dirt going through the same motions with a stick. After a while people just left him alone. Eventually he was taken to an army shrink and was put in front of a medical review board. Not only had his pattern of behaviour remained the same but he became dirty and completely silent. He was discharged, but not into freedom – he was "sectioned" and institutionalised. At some point acting mad had become an extreme hyper-obsessive-compulsive disorder. "Madness" can be created.

Sanity and madness are not completely distinct and divided states of mind. They are relative, they graduate from one to the other, and circumstantially fade into and out of focus. I know that at this moment I am sane, but I also live with the sense that at times I am probably not.

Acts of madness do not equate to madness, although they can prefigure it. Likewise, madness has been described not as a condition of dysfunction but as a way of coping with it. Whatever definition of madness is presented there is a contradictory view. Yet no matter the definition, overt acts of madness are recognisable.

The concealment of who my mother was got easier as I grew older simply because parents play a less significant part in most people's lives as they mature. Fewer questions are asked about them. Of course, I could have lied, but didn't. Just to read, think, talk or write about madness brings my mother's shadow near. The idea of madness and my mother are one. Such thoughts and feelings are obviously beyond reason and they fold back into questions of madness, which were ever lingering. I learnt to live with this. As for my own question as to whether my mother was mad or not, I have a clear answer, but it's not based upon science. As far as I am concerned, she was mad.

When I ask whether or not madness is my destiny, my answer is now 98.5 percent, *No*. If I had gone mad, I think it would have happened by now. I say this with the qualification that I still have a left-over 1.5 percent of lingering doubt.

My view of my mother's madness is based upon her actions in the world, rather than a diagnosis of her condition of mind. What these actions evidenced is open to a variety of medical interpretations, but no matter how they vary, I believe none would suggest she was of sound mind. For the most part we act on the basis of the evidence before us: if the actions of Tom are those of a madman, then Tom is mad. What we know in theory almost never overrides our direct experience. For instance, we may concur with Einstein that space, time and speed exist in a way that is relative to one another, and we may understand that we do not function independently of the laws of physics, but we do not live and act according to this knowledge. We take it in good faith, not being able to prove it otherwise, and move on. Dealing with madness is the same: faced with someone behaving in a totally crazy way one acts on the basis of what is occurring, not on one's limited or extensive theoretical knowledge of mental disorders.

Many times I have wondered if my mother's violence, cruelty and apparent sadomasochism were understandable as psychotic, or psychopathic actions. My reflections on this question were totally overshadowed by thinking about the consequences of her actions upon other people's lives. Besides the long-lasting physical damage she inflicted, and the circumstances in which it was done, she certainly did a great deal of long-lasting mental harm. Placed in this setting, madness should not only be viewed as an individual mental illness but as an environmental condition contaminating individuals, made inappropriately powerful, who abused and mistreated people over whom they were given power. Caught up in a malformed culture wherein abusive actions become a benchmark of normality, it is not surprising that madness followed. Although I cannot confirm the claim, I expect that nobody surpassed the physical and sexual atrocities carried out by my mother.

Making sense of mental illness – something that is beyond sense – is hard. Over the years my views have moved between clarity and confusion, as expert opinions have altered and professional divisions have increased. If we look at the extremes there is one medical camp that takes mental illness to be a product of nature malfunctioning at, for instance, the level of brain chemistry, or as a consequence of congenital defects and brain damage. Another camp deems that mental illness is a cultural and social construction that takes different forms according to culture, history, and arbitrary designation of norms. Then, coming from outside the psychiatric profession, there is a critical view within philosophy that sees the designation of madness as centring on restriction of freedoms of difference, the exercise of social control, a particular theory of knowledge and the exercise of the power of a normative order. Essentially all such modes of classification are based upon a bounded model of conformist human behaviour, with the policing of this boundary and the management of mechanisms of imposed conformity all denoting a society that institutionalises difference.

From inside the discourses of clinical psychology, psychiatry and psychoanalysis there are varied positions ranging from scientific classifications of specific conditions to those that say there is no objective way of clinically defining a mental condition, and no consensus on the meaning of the terminology used outside a particular subjective clinical/discursive practice of interpretation. Moreover, there is no precision in the definition of symptoms and their meanings. As for treatment, so often what occurs is the chemical suppression of symptoms in order to establish a condition of behaviour control, stability and, if possible, social function, or at worst, institutionalised patient management.

All this leaves the interested observer with an impossible task of distinguishing between the reality of non-conforming behaviours, and the conventions by which they are viewed and designated across the conduct of a subject diagnosed as delusionary, manic, suffering deep neuroses, psychosis, paranoia, personality disorders and so on, due to neurological chemical imbalance, genetic defects, or neurological disease. I came to the conclusion that anyone who goes to the trouble of exploring the history of the treatment of madness will find it, beyond superficial appearances, to be just as mad as madness itself.

Bridging these outside/inside viewpoints has been a recent recognition that, notwithstanding how Magnetic Resonance Imaging (MRI) has informed brain science and neurobiology, and how this advance combines with the ability to sequence the human genome to tell us about the brain and its connection to mental conditions, two observations have become more clearly, more widely, and more consensually understood.

Firstly, madness is not quantifiably reducible to singular expressive forms. As being-in-the-world changes, so does madness. This means that the relationship between a condition and its classification is unstable. Secondly, madness is partly socially constructed, and its recognition, classification and treatment have been subject to a globalised, Eurocentric bias in relation to clinical symptoms. In the language of science, and in the language of the culture of others, so often the named condition goes ahead of the named.

Consider this: although there are obvious cases of madness of the "I am Jesus," "I am Attila-the-Hun," "I am Joan of Arc" level of delusion, psychiatry also acknowledges that psychosis can take forms that are private and silent. Madness may not be designated via visible signs. And a silent condition may or may not produce aberrant acts. Added to this, delusion is a relative condition able to be recognised to some degree in us all. We think we are free when we are not; we think we are witty when nobody else does; we think we are unloved but we are – and so on. We live in a world of illusion and delusion – things are never what they seem. So, is it fair to expect the "us" to be any different from the "them" – the "mad"? Is it not the case that madness is a relative condition common to all of us to some degree, that only gets named in its excessive forms? Don't we all do mad things from time to time?

The point is that a continuum of life-world situations is often coped with by resort to delusion. Frequently, the line drawn between the real and the imaginary is no more than arbitrary, and often impossible to find. We all know people whose self-delusions seem out of hand, but we don't regard them as mad. I was struck by reading that Jacques Lacan, an influential radical thinker in psychiatry and psychoanalysis, held the view that James Joyce was psychotic and that this was the foundation of his celebrated creativity. Can one be creative and sane? Likewise, in a world where acts of madness by seemingly rational people and governments are constant and legion, how does one retain one's sanity?

My mother's delusion was that she was saving Germany by the elimination of Jews: her individual madness fused with that of Nazi ideology to form a deadly cocktail. Likewise, was dropping an atomic bomb on Hiroshima an act of sanity? One can argue strongly that both were wrong, but "wrong" recognised as evil is not the same as "mad." And as for mad, there is good mad and bad mad, and such thinking leads to another question.

How can violence and cruelty be viewed? Historically there have been many who have argued that violent and cruel action can be expedient. The claim is that the suffering of the few (or not so few – Hiroshima?) is justified if it saves the suffering of the many. But where is the dividing line between violence and psychopathic behaviour? Here we instantly fold back once more into the problematic issue of mental illness as a social, not an individual condition. An authoritative voice of power will always arrive to pronounce judgment. The problem is that many of these judgments will be contradictory. Notwithstanding the illusion of an objective voice, any notion of distance between myself and what I am writing about needs to be dispelled. I'm still writing in the shadow of my mother.

Sometimes the obvious takes a long time to arrive, and needs prompting to do so. This was the case when I thought about my mother and madness and the possibility of her being a psychopath. The professional view was divided on whether or not psychopathy was a condition of insanity. The answer is probably yes, but I still had doubts. On the issue of criminal insanity, the key issue was, "Did the person committing a crime know what they were doing?" And then, if what is seen to be an insane act is conducted with the application of reason, where is the line between sanity and insanity drawn? This question led me to a book on criminal insanity by psychologist Stephen McCraig.

McCraig worked in institutions for the criminally insane for thirty-two years. On retirement he wrote *Inside Forever*, a book that gave an account of his experience. In writing about the people he treated, using methods that were more about chemical restraint than cure, I recognised many qualities and characteristics that my mother appeared to have displayed, especially in terms of psychopathology and personality disorders. The obvious arrived and then instantly vanished. First, I concluded that my mother was intrinsically, or had become, criminally insane. But then the classification asserted itself as just another term, one that said everything and nothing. It thus required treatment as a question rather than an answer.

I tracked down two possible people I could talk to about the issue. Cal Johanson was a professor of criminal justice at my university whom I had met a number of times. I heard him talk about his work on institutional forms of treatment with violent prisoners. Amanda De Soto was a young senior research fellow in psychology married to a colleague of mine. I met her a couple of times at school social functions. I remembered her telling me in one of our conversations that she was working on the psychopathology of female violence.

I contacted Cal and Amanda. A few days later I met Amanda over coffee. She told me that criminal insanity was not an area she was familiar with. Nonetheless we had an interesting chat. Cal was a different story. I told him I was researching the philosophical understanding of madness and wanted to find out more about the treatment of the criminally insane. He said the best thing I could do was visit a doctor working in a hospital for the criminally insane. He had a friend working in such a place in California. He could informally arrange contact, but I would then need to make a formal application to the director of the institution. Additionally, a supporting letter from Cal and from his friend would be needed, saying he was willing to meet and take responsibility for me. Cal said it was possible a background check would be run before approval was given.

I got approval. The process took eight weeks and came with a list of restrictions. No photography was allowed and it was forbidden to enter the institution with a camera; I would be provided with an escort and could not separate from him or her at any time within the institution. Additionally, I was forbidden to mention the names of either patients or staff. My visit would be between 2.00 and 4.00pm and I had to make an appointment at least seven days prior to the visit.

I made an appointment and flew to San Francisco three weeks after getting the approval. The institution was the Department of State Hospital, Napa. I picked up a hire car at the airport. It was an easy drive to Napa. The setting of the mental institution was beautiful. Its site was selected in the nineteenth century on the understanding that the location had morally and therapeutically uplifting qualities. But its location was where the beauty ended. The place was huge: surrounded by a security fence topped with razor wire, lighting towers, an institutional administration building, security systems, and wards of varying security as high as it can get.

Cal's friend, who I will call Marco, met me at reception and signed me in. He was a thin, tall man, maybe in his mid-40s, with a warm smile that broke across a clearly a tired face, topped by tightly curled grey hair. He said he was my escort, but was having a bad day and could only give me seventy-five minutes, rather the full time I booked. He had a crisis meeting he had to attend.

He knew I was only interested in the criminally insane, which the hospital classified as "people not guilty by reason of insanity." These people were detained for an equivalent period to the sentence for the crime they had committed – on the basis of a remote chance of a cure – but in almost all cases detention was for the duration of their life. The institution's hard-core population of six hundred was held in the secure wing of the hospital. Many were extremely dangerous and individually confined. After passing through a rigorous screening process, Marco took me on a tour of the high security area where he and his team worked. It looked, felt and smelt like a prison. It was a mix of single patient confinement cells and a less foreboding social area for stable, medicated and non-dangerous inmates. I saw a mixture of people who looked perfectly normal, others who were clearly on medication, and a smaller number who were isolated and, in some way, distressed; these patients could be seen via a small, thick plexiglass window.

We walked and talked. Marco made it clear that many patients are treatable, but many are not. "They simply have to be managed so that they do not harm themselves or anyone else," he said. The staff mostly, but not always, managed to do this. He said there were some who were a challenge to medicate. "Get it wrong and these patients rave and become violent at the slightest provocation." We had a brief conversation about the narrow divide between madness, sanity and genius, about which he said: "There are some extraordinary people here. For example, we have a former doctoral student working in pure math, who spends all day every day working on problems, filling vast numbers of notebooks. We had a look at one of them while he was showering. While we couldn't make any sense of it, it was full of complex calculations. In fact, we photocopied a few pages and got a professor of math at UCSF to look over them. He said while his ideas were strange, they were rational and very obviously the product of someone with a very developed mathematical imagination. The problem was that he believed he was surrounded by people trying to steal his ideas, and as a student had violently attacked a professor and five other students with a hammer during a seminar. It was discovered he had often come to class with it hidden in the waistband of his trousers and covered by a sweater.

We also talked about an ex-policeman who, in the early 1960s, lived a Hollywood movie revenge fantasy. He sought out criminals, especially sex offenders, killing them and mutilating their bodies. He killed twelve people over two years. Apparently, he seemed normal, and nobody noticed he was strange, until one day in the station house when he saw a colleague bring in a male prostitute he was looking for. He pulled out his gun and shot the man. When his apartment was searched, the walls were covered in religious images with an altar in the living room. He believed himself to be a God-appointed avenging angel, and still does. He had "devoted himself to God" and spent his life in prayer, reading the Bible and raging against sinners of the flesh. Marco said, "He never gives the staff any trouble, but he has twice attacked another patient."

One of the strangest people Marco told me about was a man who once worked for a radio station. "The guy hosted a late-night music show playing pretty average middle-of-the-road pop. He started drinking at work and ended up doing a show drunk, got fired and totally flipped. The next night, he petrol-bombed the radio station. He then started bombing record stores around town. When he was caught and taken into custody, he just talked hate-filled gibberish. The way he now talks is as if he is still at the mic at his radio station studio desk."

We also discussed violent sexual offenders whose fantasies led them to unbelievable perverted savagery that mostly never got into the media. Again, the scary thing about many of these people is that they can and do present themselves as normal rational human beings. They are actors skilled in self-concealment. Finally, Marco said, "With dangerous people who act dangerously you know what you're dealing with. It's those who are dangerous, but appear normal, rational, coherent, and under control, who are the real danger. Being insane does not always mean that you cannot plan, reason and act. The cunning of some of these people can be amazing."

Marco and I sat in his office drinking coffee and talking about the constant rise in hospital admissions, until he realised he had to go to his meeting. He walked me back to reception to sign out. On the way I asked him how he coped. His answer reflected his tiredness. "Mostly I just do, sometimes I don't and today it's borderline." I had not arrived on the best of days. I thanked him profusely before leaving and got a big smile. He gave me an envelope that he said contained information about the place that I might find interesting. It was an unforgettable hour and a half. "Marco" was a memorable person.

As I drove back to San Francisco, my head was spinning. What had I learnt? What did I need to learn? And above all, what connections could I make to my mother? Was I convinced she was criminally insane? From everything I saw, had been told and read, I saw commonalities and differences, but concluded that the probability was that she was at least a psychopath, or had become criminally insane. Having read a little about this condition, and talked to Marco, not only did I now understand that it was graduated, but that I had some psychopathic traits. This did not mean that I was a danger to society, but I recognised that I lacked empathy. This realisation prompted a back-reading of my relations with colleagues and students. While I believe I showed consideration, I felt that my actions displayed a lack of comprehension of the effect of what I said. I had no feeling of hurting other people's feelings, when sometimes I did. Was this trait inherited? Maybe. Was it a consequence of my withdrawal largely into a world of my own, and my concealment of my dark secret from absolutely everyone? Maybe. Whatever the answers, I knew I would take this trait as a mark of likeness to my mother.

Although I could and did deal with such knowledge of myself, it still disturbed me. I knew that in comparative terms, my psychopathic state was very mild and manageable. The fact that I had this knowledge prompted a greater conscious application of self-reflection and care in dealing with others, so I viewed the knowledge as the silver lining of the cloud in which I dwelt.

I did not open the envelope Marco gave me until I was on the plane back to New York. Mostly it was a history of the foundation of the hospital and its changes and dramas over the years. But there was also some descriptive information that gave me a better perspective on the place and its scale – it had around 1,100 beds and over 2,000 staff. There were three other areas in addition to the one I visited. One was called "Civil Committee," and was for individuals who, due to their mental illness, were deemed to be a danger to themselves or others. A second was for people "incompetent to stand trial," who were subject to assessment and treatment prior to being returned to court for a final trial ruling. The other area of the hospital was for "mentally disturbed offenders" who had committed a crime, been convicted and were held and treated as a condition of their parole.

My recall of that flight home is still vivid. It was thought-provoking and uncomfortable but above all, transformative. Confronting madness and mental conditions abstractly as words on the page is one thing. Actually, being in an institution surrounded by the mentally ill and talking to the extraordinary people who deal with them every day are totally different. I was a little frustrated that I had not had time to discuss sadomasochism. But I had fewer doubts about my mother on that count. By the time we arrived in New York I knew my understanding had altered just a little, but, above all, my proximity to her had changed. She might not have accepted me into her life as her child, and so erased my presence in the days she had left, but I now accepted her as my mother. Somehow, a space had opened for me between her fundamental being and her mind and actions. Like all monstrous people, their monstrosity was overwhelmed by the sadness of their condition. This is what I saw when I looked through the plexiglass at those distressed people with damaged minds locked in their awful rooms.

Where once I saw a photograph of a beautiful and evil young woman, I now saw an image of pure sadness: a human being gripped by the hand of fate and the demonic forces of a despicable regime.

Because we had not discussed sadomasochism at Napa, on the evening of my return to Stony Brook I re-read my notes. I had recorded three major observations. First, there is a general opinion among those in social and medical professions who deal with sadomasochism that it is directly related to the experiences a child has during its early sexual development – this is said to have a profound effect upon the formation of their sexual character as an adult. I wonder about my mother's childhood, and in particular her relations with her father and brothers. Second, sadomasochism is made up of two conditions that can exist independently or together – sadism and masochism. (Sadism is the sexual emphasis, masochism is the pleasure from giving or receiving pain; sadomasochism is sexual pleasure acquired from pain.) The unity of these conditions is consistent with descriptions of my mother's conduct. And third is the observation that, when moved into the realm of mental illness, the fantasies, deviant urges and behaviour only become social problems when they create clinically identifiable distress and dysfunction within forms of social exchange in everyday life.

Unquestionably this was true in my mother's case. Consider the numerous accounts of her behaviour: beating the faces of young women to destroy their looks, slashing the breasts of young women, forcing young women to have sex with her and then making sure they ended up in the gas chamber, having orgasms while beating prisoners. It would seem she was a sadomasochist in the extreme. Her frightful activities were beyond the imagination of de Sade. The gross visceral nature and cruelty of her actions do not reside in the realm of reason.

13

The Day the World Turned

It will hardly come as a surprise to learn that from my teens I wondered about other people who were the children of truly monstrous parents. There would only be a handful of us. In my thirties I started to search. The problem was not just discovering who these people were but finding anything in detail about them. I assumed that like me, almost all of them lived by gatekeeping their history, thus ensuring that their secret remained secure and protected. As I discovered, these people were reluctant to say anything about themselves and especially about their parents. In the end I found two people whose stories were significant, and who were willing to talk to me.

The first of these was Berlin flower seller Uta Beckermann. I discovered her by chance when watching a documentary film. But before telling these people's stories, I want to say that, while searching, I discovered something that had a profound and disturbing effect upon me. Most academics discover things by organised and rigorous research, but occasionally serendipity lends a hand. While looking for something else suddenly and by accident an important discovery is made. It can be while browsing in a bookstore, searching an archive box in a library, on the Internet, or even by catching sight of a paper on the desk of a colleague. In this case I was on the way home from a conference in Charlotte, Virginia. Like so many times before, I had time to kill at the airport and was in the bookstore flicking through a magazine. My eye caught a bright and seemingly abstract cover on *Scientific American*. I've no idea what it was. I picked the magazine up, casually turned a few pages and was hit by a headline that paralysed me: "Scientists Discover Children's Cells Living in Mothers' Brains." The words tipped my world off its axis.

The essence of the research was that the link between a mother and child was far stronger than anyone realised, both physically and psychologically. Actual bonds were formed during the gestation period when a mother was the total environment of the fetus and supplied its vital nourishment. The placenta was an organ of two-way exchange, and cells migrated through it. What blew my mind was that not only do cells from the fetus find their way into the mother's body, but cells from the mother take up residence in almost all organs of the fetus. Besides the genetic inheritance from both parents, at a cellular level, a physical trace of our mother lives in us, including in our brain.

It's hard to communicate how I felt. The intellectual realisation was that there was more than a genetic connection to my mother because, in addition to this, bits of her became part of me. Her cells were inside me; she had contaminated me. In the space of a few seconds, I felt disgusted, defiled, angry, panic-stricken, and, above all, frightened. If I had read the article when I was in my twenties, I doubt I could have gone on. But now I had an anchor in the fact that I survived, and could continue to survive. I had a history that, compared to hers, was "normal." Nonetheless everything changed. Internally I perceived myself as being inhabited by another. I felt different. I had an invisible deformity delivered by an alien. This is a retrospective view. At the time, after my first reaction, I did a temporary inversion of the line from Timothy Leary who said, "Turn on, tune in, drop out". I entered a state like that conferred by the drug Mogadon: I turned off, went silent, disappeared. I slept for a week, disconnected. By the second week I regained some level of functionality and by week three I was almost okay. In the company of the alien within me, my disturbed life moved on.

Berlin flower seller Uta Beckermann, the other person I visited was a man called Ernst von Schroder. Both lived alone: she modestly and he in abject poverty in a huge crumbling country house in Lower Saxony. The house, he proudly told me, was built in the mid-eighteenth century and was the jewel of an estate that was the property of the wealthy, aristocratic, land-owning 'von Schroder' family. The house was the last vestige of the estate, the farming land having been sold many decades ago. I read about von Schroder in a German travel magazine when I looked for material on Wrechen. The article was more about the village and the house than about him, but after discovering Ernst I went looking for, and found, information about his father. The more research I did on the men, the more interesting the story of this senior Nazi party member became.

I went to a British film festival in New York with Karen during a long weekend. I learnt from her that there was a BBC documentary on children and other close relatives of Nazi war criminals in the program. It was an excellent film, mostly about the infamous. For instance, Rainer Hoess told what it was like to be the grandson of the first commandant of Auschwitz. There were accounts from the daughter of Amon Goeth, the sadistic commandant of Plaszow concentration camp. She talked about being brought up in her mother's fantasy world of goodness and light. Katrina Himmler then gave a guided tour of the multiple branches of her Nazi family tree. Next came an interview with Bettina Goering who, along with her brother, chose to be sterilised to break the bloodline from her father. During the film there was also a very short interview with Uta Beckermann, the daughter of Horst Beckermann, a notorious guard at the Mauthausen work camp. I identified with her more than with the others. She was down-to-earth, and what she said was not staged; her narrative was not scripted.

That Uta's father had been at Mauthausen interested me: I had read about the place. It was created with two objectives, one being the quarrying of stone for Hitler's megalomaniac architectural fantasies designed by Albert Speer. The other, in the spirit of the ironic death camp slogan, "Arbeit Mach Frei," was as a camp where prisoners *en masse* were literally worked to death. Beckermann was tried and hanged in 1946 after confessing to beating numerous prisoners to death when they fell carrying rocks up the 186 "steps of death." He did this when the men were no longer able to get to their feet. He was also implicated in other brutal acts including, in the depths of the winter, stripping prisoners naked, spraying them with water, and watching them freeze to death.

When I got home from the film festival, I spent time tracking down Paul Kennedy, the journalist who worked on the film and interviewed Uta. I got his number and, after a brief phone conversation, I decided to go to London to talk to him. If things worked out, I would go on to Germany and see Uta.

We met in a coffee shop in Earls Court and talked for over an hour. I expected him to be cagey, but he was open and helpful – so this was an unexpected surprise. We discussed the people he interviewed including Uta. I called him the next day and said I would like to make contact with Uta, making a case why this was important to me "for the book." He reluctantly gave me her details. I also wanted to visit Ernst von Schroder if he was still alive. I knew where his village was and doubted that he would be hard to find.

From her interview and my conversation with Paul Kennedy, I knew Uta was eight years old in 1946, and had a brother who was eleven. Kennedy told me that Russian soldiers raped the brother in front of her when he was ten, and at the age of fifteen he committed suicide. Their mother abandoned them both in 1947, and was never heard of again. Uta lived for two years with one of the bands of orphans that roamed the streets of Berlin after its fall. Then fate took a hand in her life. After stealing a bag from an unlocked car, she discovered it contained a Voigtländer camera. She immediately sold it and bought food and flowers. She was smart and remembered seeing a young woman in a wheelchair selling cut flowers from a bucket and decided she would become a street flower seller. She knew she could find flowers in graveyards, parks and abandoned gardens, and with a few tin cans and some water she managed to create a meagre income stream. By 1959 she was renting a small shop on *Wilmersham Straße* and was operating as a florist. She still has the same business in the same place. She lives on her own in a one-bedroom apartment that she bought in 1974. Kennedy told me that she was friendly with many of the local shopkeepers and some of her customers had been buying her flowers for years.

I visited Uta at her shop and told her I wanted to chat after seeing her BBC TV interview. She said, "I didn't like doing it. They left a lot out and made me look old." I held back a smile. We talked about the film for a few minutes and then I asked about her father. She said, "I am a daughter of the devil, and I have spent my life trying to forget him." I said I was also a devil's daughter and that my mother was a guard at Bergen-Belsen, one of the worst, who was executed in 1946. Uta said nothing but just touched the side of my face with the back of her hand. When I asked about her life, she slowly turned with arms outstretched and said "You're looking at it; this is all the life I got." It was hard to get her to say much about her father – "I never really knew him, he was never at home, so I know nothing about him except what he got hung for." The person she wanted to talk about was her brother.

She still missed him and prayed for him every night. What she wished for more than anything was a photograph of him, as she couldn't remember what he looked like. Tears flowed slowly into the creases of her face; she trembled and I held her. I told her I had no one and wished I had a brother. We cried together; she was still shaking and felt so frail. I honestly thought she was going to die in my arms. But then a customer, a young woman, arrived to buy a single white rose. Uta stepped back, nodded her head at me. That was it. The moment and our meeting was over. I touched her arm and left. I went back to my hotel knowing I would never see her again. I was filled with sadness but, for the first time in my life, I felt I was no longer on my own. The only thing I wanted to do was sleep.

When following up on Ernst von Schroder I came across a review of a book on Himmler by the historian, Walter Kruss, in which von Schroder's father figured. I tracked the book down. It gave attention to the part Himmler played in the elimination of the Jewish population of Poland. During this, Kruss discussed the friendship between Himmler and SS-Brigadefuher Schroder, who was the most important regional governor in Poland and the authority who promulgated orders that led to the death of tens of thousands of Jews. Kruss wrote off the efforts of von Schroder's eldest son Ernst to exonerate the actions of his father.

What interested me was how to make sense of an offspring of a war criminal who, in contrast to almost all of his peers, rather than recoiling from the parent's actions, rallied to his defence. Secondly, I was aware, as were those judges who tried war criminals, that the written directives to kill Jews issued from a T4 office in Berlin, Poland, or elsewhere, were just as lethal as a bullet in the head. I wondered if Ernst was refusing to recognise this and formed a view, via a self-authored illusion, wherein he believed his father did not actually have blood on his hands.

Getting Ernst von Schroder's address was easy: I simply looked him up in a telephone directory. I wrote to him two months before leaving home, said I planned to do research on the offspring of convicted World War Two war criminals when I came to Germany, and asked if he would allow me to interview him. I got a reply three weeks later in a letter with a crest twice the size of the message written in an elegant script. It simply said, "Delighted, give me at least a week's notice," followed by his telephone number, which I already had.

I called him from Berlin the day after I met Uta. I spent a few more days in Berlin, then hired a car and drove to Hanover for the weekend and then up to von Schroder's house in Walsrode, a few miles outside the town. The prospect of the visit made me uneasy. I was in my mother's land. Walsrode was not far from Bergen-Belsen (no longer a name on the map) and Wrechen was only a few more hours away. Was this the moment to visit the camp? I wasn't sure. I decided I would wait and see how I felt after the interview.

Ernst was waiting at the gate to greet me. He must have been there for some time because all I said was that I would arrive mid-to-late morning. I arrived at 11.45. He held out his hand to shake mine. His grip was surprisingly strong, although he looked frail. The path from the gate to the house was over one hundred metres. Ernst walked slowly, sometimes stopping, while giving me a bit more than a potted history of the family – it took us around fifteen minutes to do the walk. As we stepped over the threshold into the house the temperature dropped by about five degrees.

There was not a stick of furniture in the two rooms we passed through *en route* to a kitchen. It was large. Its floor of sandstone flagstones was worn, and in the middle stood a huge, heavy pine table with wooden benches along both sides. Behind it a well-stoked but ancient kitchen range warmed the room. I doubt if anything had changed for a century or more. Ernst offered me coffee. I gratefully accepted and handed him a small box of assorted cakes that we could share. From the look on his face, it was evident that such treats were infrequent. It took another half an hour of chatting before we got to the conversation I'd come for. As soon as I said I wanted to ask him a few questions, Ernst became discernibly nervous. Before I had a chance to pose the first question, he told me that his father was a "fine man" and from a shelf under the table he produced a framed photograph of the family gathered around his father. "This is me." He looked about four or five years old. "Not only was my father a fine man he was also a good man." That gave me a way in: "Do you mean he was good to you, or good to everyone?" His reply wrong-footed me: "Are you trying to trick me?" Before I could reply, he said, "I know there was good inside my father and I have to find it, I have to." We sat in silence for what seemed an age but couldn't have been more than a minute. Then I asked: "What do you remember about your father?" His reply was instant, animated and long: "I remember we were a family and he loved us. The family was destroyed, they spat at us; they would not serve us in the shops. One day some boys from the village threw bags of dog shit at my mother. She left us on the same day, taking my two sisters with her. I never saw or heard from them again. My brother, Carl, and I went to live with my grandmother who sent us to a boarding school in Hamburg; this was when I was nine." Ernst was six years old in 1945 when he last saw his father. "Did you marry?" "No." "What about Carl? "I don't want to talk about Carl, he's not here, he went." Alone and poor, Ernst's father was all there was for him.

"Why do you think your father did what he did?" "He did it for Germany, he did it because he was ordered to do it." I waited a moment. "But what he did was wrong." Ernst banged the table: "It was going to happen anyway, he didn't give the orders, he did as he was instructed and signed the papers. If he hadn't, someone else would have. They would have been just as guilty as him!" The old man was shouting. I pointed out that the judges at the trial had no doubt about his father's guilt: "As evidence, they had the documents he signed, that sent thousands of people to their death." Ernst looked distressed: "I don't know, I don't know, he was my father, but what I do know was that he was a good man, a good German."

It was pointless to continue. I tried to think how to extricate myself from the situation, but Ernst did it for me: "Where are you going next?" I told him I was going back to Berlin and then flying out the next day. We talked briefly about Berlin; he told me how it once was a great city. I thanked him and left.

The experience was disconcerting and rather tragic. It seemed like a wasted effort, but looking back it wasn't. I discovered a significant lesson. There was something worse than shutting out an "evil" parent from one's life, and that was letting them in. My life had been painful. Ernst's life had been empty. He survived by selling off parts of the estate until it was all gone, then he moved on to disposing of the antique furniture. Judging by appearances, his life had been an endless process of loss, in significant part because of his misplaced attachment to his father, an illusion to fill the void.

I could have done a quick detour to Bergen-Belsen and Celle *en route* to Berlin, but decided not to. I would do it another day.

14

The Problem of the Limits

When I got home from Germany, I spent a good deal of time reflecting on the experience. As ever, with everything associated with my mother and my life, the emotional and intellectual always collided. Whatever I discovered I tried to make sense of as both experience and feelings.

Uta, Ernst and I could not have been more different, yet we had something that made us the same. Our lives were destroyed by the actions of a parent against others; we were another item of their collateral damage. We were unable to break the bond to the parental past that framed our lives. Uta lived the presence of that devil that was her father; Ernst devoted his life to a negation of what his father was and did, and so had no life of his own. I was trapped by the questions that my mother left me with – questions that I have said so much about. In many ways she was nothing but these questions. It could not be otherwise. I had almost no knowledge of her beyond what was in the public domain and what was biologically discoverable. I was a host to some of her cells.

My process of reflection did not stay still. It jumped about: my thoughts and feelings moved between clarity and confusion. In an instant I moved between thinking about myself, Germany, my mother, the irrational fears I harboured, the past, the future, music and death. Slowly the mental and emotional noise quietened and clarity started to form. This peace could last for days or weeks, but something – a remark, an image or memory – shattered it.

While my parents and those of Uta and Ernst were different they shared the lie of believing in the Nazi cause, and that its leaders directed them to do what they did for the benefit of the Third Reich. Equally, they were emotionally immune to the consequences of their actions, not least in inflicting pain on others. On this, I'm not sure about Ernst's father, but certainly my mother and Uta's father gained visceral pleasure from doing so. I believe they gained a psychological frisson from the ability to exercise power over the fate of powerless human beings.

I again reflected on the ways I viewed my mother as mad, the issue of "madness," and the whole Nazi project itself as a huge moment of collective insanity. Here was a project wherein reason was continuously deployed in the service of something completely and utterly irrational. I knew this before the trip to Germany, but didn't feel it strongly until I was there. What I realised was that collective insanity was not just a flaw within the Nazi regime but one, as Nietzsche knew, inherent in modernity in itself. The service of reason to advance irrationality folded into modernity in general and into war in particular. This realisation gave added poignancy to Nietzsche's declaration that "the world is mad." I really felt, and still feel, that humanity is self-destructively out of control. Thinking, and feeling the angst of this judgment brought me back to the relationship between excess and evil as a material, rather than moral, issue.

I needed to talk to someone. I wanted to test my state of mind by voicing my opinions then gauging the responses and reactions of another person. My thoughts turned to Christopher. He would instantly see the psychological connection. I knew his reactions would be honest. He would be able to understand how I felt. But I was hesitant: is this how I wanted him to see me? Would being open with him compromise my self-protection? How could I say what I wanted to say? What were the elements of the collective insanity that sucked in so many sane people? In the end I just put the idea of talking to him on hold.

Unannounced, a book arrived. It was a present from a former student who landed a job teaching in a film school in Sydney. I remember the book as a drab-looking, thin volume based on a lecture the postmodern theorist, Jean Baudrillard, gave at an Australian university. The attractor was the title: "The Evil Demon of Images". My pondering on the question of sanity must have triggered a connection with the title. First it echoed the images of my mother, then it related to the whole spectacle of Nazi Germany, "that proud and glorious nation that arose from a dream of ancient Greece," liberated from the politics of shame and humiliation experienced by *"der volk"* post-World War One. The dream, as it turned into the modern spectacle, was theorised at the time by Seigfried Kracauer in his book, *The Mass Ornament*. The underpinning idea of the evil image was captured and explored by Guy Debord in his 1960s work, *Society of the Spectacle*. These books are an overt recognition of the seduction of "the masses" by an image that incited an insane desire and became a directive towards action to realise its promise.

The notion that Baudrillard evoked and examined drew on the work of Marshall McLuhan, who argued that the power of the image as evil and demonic has not diminished; it just shifted its attachment from fascism to late capitalism and hyper-consumerism. In Nazi Germany the spectral form of the demon arrived full-blown with the pomp of huge parades, striking uniforms, flags, drums, mass events, in spectacular settings, orchestrated by the possessed Fuhrer, the shaman Adolf Hitler. His ranting came with the same forceful subtext espoused by all dangerous leaders: simple solutions to complex problems, attached to an available scapegoat to blame and purge as the designated cause of the nation's problems. As is often forgotten, this was by no means the first time in the history of Europe that the Jews were depicted by a regime as an enemy to be dealt with by expulsion or elimination. The irrational rise of Fascist Germany begs re-emphasis as it progressed by the application of highly organised and well-disciplined rational means. Doubters were carried along helplessly by the hate machine of the militarised state with its elevation of racism as a spectral national ideology. It was far more complex than I'm suggesting. In spite of this, at no other moment in human history was aesthetic power unquestionably mobilised to seduce and deploy the masses for ill rather than good. This was enabled by a perversely demonic appeal to people who desperately sought the restoration of national pride and a better material future.

In trying to make sense of the Nazi use of the symbolic in the service of the irrational, I went looking for a source. In the end I found it referenced in a document created in 1942 by the British intelligence service. The document was recently, and accidently, discovered by a researcher working in a Cambridge library.

The original document was written by a social scientist, Mark Abrams, who was attached to the psychological warfare division of the allied expeditionary force. The document's discovery became the basis of a story in Britain's *Guardian* newspaper. From this lead I was able to track the document down. What I discovered was that its analysis in 1942 supported the view of Hitler as a shaman.

What Abrams did was to undertake a detailed analysis of a speech delivered by Hitler on April 26, 1942. In this speech he began with a diatribe against the Jews as the harbingers of pure evil while characterising himself as the champion of "the good." He then reflected on the campaign in Russia. It was already becoming clear, as Abrams pointed out, that Hitler's prediction of victory and the annihilation of Russia was wrong. He realised that if Russia could not be defeated and Britain could not be totally blockaded by U-boats, the war would be lost. In this setting Abrams's aim was to expose Hitler's state of mind. He was prompted to do this on the basis that in January there had been press reports of Hitler's "morbid tendencies."

Abrams's analysis of the text's content centred on three figures that Abrams believed underpinned Hitler's conduct: the shaman, the epileptic, and the paranoiac. The shaman creates an escalating frenzied state of being before the crowd in the belief that a vital message has to, and is, being communicated. This characterisation of Hitler's key mode of delivery "in the early phase of the war" was familiar. But Abrams goes further and notes that, increasingly during the war, Hitler's hysterical oratory skills declined and his voice began to sound flat and dull. Abrams connects this to the psychology of the epileptic, which he defines in various ways, including with links to behavioural problems such as impatience and, when frustrated, loss of interest. While contemporary medical opinion may have reservations about Abrams's views, it supports his claims that some sufferers of epilepsy are prone to psychological problems. Was Hitler an epileptic? While it was not widely acknowledged publicly, it seems it was known. For example, tucked away in the *London Evening Standard* of 19 July 1941 we find the following headline and report:

HITLER REPORTED TO HAVE
HAD EPILEPTIC FIT

London, Today.
Moscow radio last night quoted informed circles in Berne for a report that a number of famous German doctors had been summoned to Berchtesgaden as a result of Hitler having suffered an epileptic fit during a military conference. The Berlin radio replied by announcing that Hitler on Friday received two airmen and decorated them with the Iron Cross.

Abrams points to the third characteristic, paranoia, expressed via Hitler's sense of himself as a messiah leading the German people to a "successful crusade against the forces of evil", the Jews. It hardly requires a qualification in psychology to recognise that such an ambition was an extreme manifestation of a religious delusion, together with a perverse notion of evil. Nonetheless not only was it deployed to legitimise dehumanising conduct but, more generally, it spawned a large quasi-military subculture who were seduced by the image, rhetoric and message espoused by Hitler. Added to this, and perhaps supporting it, is the recent revelation that Hitler was addicted to opioids.

What I started to realise more clearly was that the "evil" power of the image had the ability to overwhelm the mind, and that it could inhabit and seduce imaginations, independently of its aesthetic character or genre. The images of my mother, again, reasserted their power to haunt.

Once more I spent hours trying to see beyond what was evident in images of my mother, in the knowledge that she saw the Jews exactly as Hitler had projected them. I realised that seeing them as less than human was not an attitude that originated with Hitler's project and representational practices. Such a characterisation of the Jews, as I've acknowledged, receded back in time as a continuous stream of personified evil within European history. What constructed my mother's vision of what was "absolutely obvious" was fed by this long history. All the Nazis did was tap into it, modernise it and nourish it with a hyper-dose of hatred and an iconography.

As a result of becoming increasingly interested in this area, I now found myself back in the library trying to discover, and make sense of, the history of anti-Semitism. The story is long, as the following summary shows. The more I read, the more devastating the story became. I came to recognise that the Holocaust was just one moment in a continuum rather than being a discrete event.

Anti-Semitism is said to have started in Egypt around 2,300 years ago, and continued unabated for several centuries (that's when it is claimed to have been first recorded). One thousand years before this, according to the Christian Bible, Moses led the Jews out of Egypt.

One finds accounts of anti-Semitism given by both Greek and Roman scholars. But once Christianity became the state religion of Rome in the 4th century the situation of the Jews became worse. They were now exposed to a far higher level of religious intolerance and oppression by the state. This situation continued to deteriorate and culminated in the early Middle Ages with the start of the Crusades in 1096. Jewish communities were destroyed and hundreds of thousands were expelled from Western Europe. Famously, these events culminated, as mentioned earlier, with the expulsion of Jews from Spain in 1492. I discovered that Martin Luther was a vehement Jew-hater who wrote a pamphlet in 1543 titled, *On the Jews and Their Lies*, in which he urged a pogrom against them, and argued for their permanent oppression. This anti-Semitic culture was embraced and promoted by Lutherans, especially in the area that is now modern-day Germany.

Anti-Semitism continued throughout the centuries, and was especially bad in Russia. Much later, it took significant foothold in Germany and France. Then, in the mid-19th century, it was given new impetus by the racial theorists of Social Darwinism. It was during this moment that the term "anti-Semitism" was coined in 1879 by Wilhelm Marr, the founder of the League of Antisemites.

The events that unfolded in Germany in 1933 were to prefigure the Holocaust. They arrived out of, and were connected to, this long, disgraceful and painful history of anti-Semitism. The Nazis commenced their rule of terror by excluding Jews from national life, blaming them for the ills of both capitalism and communism, and then in 1935 banning marriage and sexual relationships between Jews and non-Jews. By 1938 things got worse: the reign of terror against Jews started on the 9th and 10th of November when the regime sanctioned the killing of Jews, the destruction of their property and the burning of synagogues. The infamous name given to this event was "*Kristallnacht.*"

This thread of thought started with reflections on my visit to Germany. What I have said is intended to communicate what I learnt and said to and for myself. It was a revelation. I now had my mother firmly placed in the world in which she came into being. I quake in the recognition of the destructive power amassed by humans and the still unchecked omnipresence of irrationality displayed by our species at all levels of social and political life.

15
Leadership and Guilt

In spite of spending time in Germany, and reading German texts for many years, I woke one morning with a question about Germany that pinned me to my bed as powerfully as a slab of concrete. I simply could not move.

For most of my life I had known I was German. I have an American accent, passport, home and long-time life in the US but I was still German. It was a fated legacy of unfreedom I inherited from my parents. But the banal question that held me in its grip as I awoke was one I probably had before: "What does being German mean to me?" Why did this question hit me now, and what made this particular confrontation with it different? Did it matter? I could, and at first did, invent answers, but actually there were no answers.

It was hopeless to try to think myself out of this seemingly pointless situation. I gave up. Then things started to change slowly. I realised that the question was an emotional rather than an intellectual one. I had not viewed it in this way in the past. From this new starting point, I began to feel that there was something about Germany that I wanted to identify with. What was it? Could I revise what I knew, knowing that my feelings and knowledge couldn't be separated from the darker side of the nation's recent past, and the conditions of my birth? Somehow, I felt that there was an affinity between the biological "stain" within me and the deep stain of the nation. At the same time, I did not feel the guilt carried by my generation. What I experienced was fear and shame, not guilt. We children of fascism have been unable to expunge the shame, even if we were without fear. Without any reference to myself I decided this would be the issue to talk over at a nothing-special dinner with Christopher.

Winter was just setting in, so I served a hearty stew and home baked bread. Christopher arrived on the dot of seven with a bottle of wine. He leaned against the kitchen doorjamb telling me about his visit to Stockholm the previous week. He talked, I half listened as I did a quick bench tidy, and dished up the meal.

Everything seemed to be going well; the stew was excellent, we followed up with cheese and biscuits, during which I chose my moment. I framed what I wanted to say by remarking on some recent research on nineteenth century anti-Semitism and Lutheran theology. It was part of the material that made me wonder if Germans had a historically inculcated sense of superiority, and if true, was this at the core of an intrinsic racism that still exists, even if its ugliness remains unspoken by neo-fascists on the streets? I tried to sound casual but my quietly provocative delivery came across as a little wooden and slightly tense. Nonetheless, I expected that the remarks would start a conversation. However, I got a noisy pushing around of the saltshaker accompanied by a long pause and then two words: "Heavy, heavy."

Rather than backing off I shifted my point of focus and tried to give what I mistakenly thought was a nudge forward by saying, "While it is understandable the way the Jews in Israel have militarised themselves and become the most powerful force in the Middle East, cannot this be understood on the basis that they are never again going to be defenceless in the face of an enemy that they believe would wish or try to annihilate them? Isn't the way they have dealt with Palestinians, and their containment in Gaza, strange? It seems to me to have more than a touch of the inhumanity that they themselves experienced full strength?"

Christopher's mood dramatically changed. From being unwilling to respond to my first question, other than by a dismissive rhetorical gesture, he was now irritated. I had never seen him act in this way. First of all, he sent a couple of passive-aggressive questions my way: "Is what you say really true?" And, "Have you been to Israel?" Then, with obvious disdain he said, "Surely this is one of those topics where people who are not properly informed should keep their mouths shut." I was dumbstruck. This was not the person I knew, but someone looking for a fight. As I knew he was not Jewish, I had no idea why. I had touched a raw nerve. My first thought was to retaliate, and what came into my mind was, "Are you suggesting I know nothing about the issue?" Instantly I thought better of it and simply said, "Would you like a coffee before you go?" But that was an equally dumb move. Taking it as an invitation to leave, Christopher instantly got to his feet and said "I'm gone."

A line had been crossed, but exactly what line was unclear. Time would tell, and it did. The friendship was no more. I phoned, I wrote, but was treated to complete silence. For a long time I was confused and hurt. I thought our friendship was solid, and had the view that such friendships could withstand an occasional disagreement. The hurt has healed somewhat, but the confusion remains. Was this person ever close to me, or was it all an act? Why was his reaction to the issues I raised so off-hand or even hostile? From the conversations we had over several years I had not discerned any particular political position towards Israel. What I realised was that, like me, Christopher had a secret no-go area which I now took to be absolute. If I'm correct, this makes the debacle even more tragic for us both. Whatever, the cause of the incident at the basic level just did not make sense.

I felt and feel as if my life has been a process of stumbling – or bumbling – forward. It feels as if I have moved from one question to another for which I can never find a satisfactory answer. Yet I cannot stop, even though losing a friend when I have so few made me think that my life was shrinking. How did I value this friendship's now questionable status? Were my words a product of ineptitude, a bad day, or received by Christopher in a state of depression? I would never know. What I did know was that questions about my mother could not be segregated from questions about German racism, and while quartz-hard, they provided a purpose that kept me focussed. Her actions, and those of others like her, could neither be exonerated nor forgiven, but my generation more than any other had the responsibility to confront them. We had to be a line of defence against the opening of pathways toward forgetting. These questions and issues belonged to Germany because it stands not just for the horrors of its own making but as a marker of the horrors that are latent in all nations, as events subsequent to World War Two, such as the genocidal actions of nations like Soviet Russia, Cambodia and Rwanda confirmed.

In the eyes of the world, the phenomenon of guilt linked to the acts of a nation gets expressed and abstracted in many ways, not least by the men and women, now old, who say, "I am not, and will not be held responsible for the sins of my father (or mother)." But I'm certain there is a big mismatch between what many Germans say and what they feel. Conversely, it is not only jack-booted neo-Nazis with shaved heads who espouse the return of fascism but an enduring cadre of silent, seething, be-suited neo-nationalist racists sitting on the parliamentary benches of many European nations.

All of this, and more, has been grist to the mill of a generation of German writers and artists who have taken on the task of exorcising fascism and the shedding of guilt for the acts of their fathers and mothers, with, one has to say, mixed degrees of success. Bookshop shelves are full of their work. New publications arrive all the time on every imaginable aspect of the reign of the Nazis, as do documentaries on World War Two.

In light of this history and my soul searching, I realised that the question of where I stand on what being German means is not simply my question but one for almost every German family living with a complicated relationship to the history of the nation. Some live with pride, more with residual shame, but many live in silence. Notwithstanding the power and status of contemporary Germany, there remains a bitterness in the culture, be it about Nazi rule, Russian excesses, defeat, occupation, or how the rest of the world views the nation. It may be dismissed, refused or rejected by many, especially the young, but the taste is still present. I can taste it.

From what I know, when the spirit of the 1960s was in full strength, the younger generation started to challenge and question their parents and grandparents about what they did in the war, and their relation to the rise of fascism. Many of the young did not accept the collective amnesia of the nation, nor the line that the vast majority of the German people knew nothing about the atrocities the Wehrmacht and SS committed. It now seems extraordinary that it was not until the 1970s that teaching about the Nazi period became part of school curricula and historians began to seriously research and document the rise of the Nazis.

Against the backdrop of this period, and all I've said, I still find the rise of the neo-Nazis incomprehensible. More than this, the fact that these people have a history of taking to the streets of German cities to visibly honour and celebrate Hitler as a great and inspirational leader astounds me. How could it be possible? As I have said, the fact that anti-Semitism is still alive in the land (and not just in Germany), and that fascism not only exists but increasingly participates in the political system of Europe and the Americas, seems to be an abomination that should not be tolerated in any civilised society. That a few years ago neo-Nazi parties won parliamentary seats in two German states, and thereafter continued to build popular political support, and exploit the structural disadvantage of former East Germans, is an indictment of the German state and democracy. The extraordinary renaissance of fascism in Europe is the rawest exposure of just how structurally present racism is in humanity itself. It haunts me and keeps me awake at night. It's not just that it is appalling in itself, but that so many societies globally tolerate the intolerable.

Maybe a month went by between the first and second time I asked myself "What does being German mean to me?" and those subsequent reflections of which I have just spoken. In that month something changed as a result of the collision between emotion and reason. I now think about the question differently because I actually have two questions that collide with each other: "What does being German *feel* like to me?" and "How do I *think* about being German"? As I've said, I feel the shame of having the parents I had, and feel that shame folds into how I feel about that Germany of which they were an unacceptable part. As I express this shame it arrives via a rationalised exposition. Yet it is more than this. It's part of the pain, and perhaps shame, of being unable to represent, even to myself, how I really feel. I know I am labouring the point, but like millions and millions of Germans I can say that what happened in the time of horror was not my fault. I know this to be true, but I don't believe it. I am German. To say this implies an un-chosen responsibility.

I realise that the inexplicable breakdown of my friendship with Christopher, and my inability to make sense of what happened, merged with a more general and enduring sense of lack. I lived in an unresolved situation, and this was rather like living with the emotional equivalent of an open wound that will not heal.

Being German is both an absence and a presence in my life. It has no material presence, yet it is there. It is a memory without content, a sense of attachment without anything to attach to, an affinity and something from which I recoil. These immaterialities are real and will not leave my inner life.

Even more irrationally, I know I cannot *not* be my parents' child. This has nothing to do with nation, or race, or genetics. It is everything to do with coming to terms with what they were, and cannot be divided from what made them so. Their being was erased and then recast in a mould created out of that design that was Nazi negative ontology; it cast them as "monsters." In this situation, being German is a state of mind that I have to break free from, but cannot because I have no attachment. Essentially, this is because I have an un-chosen belonging to the negative. My trip to Germany made this clearer to me. I am not alone. I am part of that mostly-by-choice childless generation who are the unspoken end of the line. Yet what is awful to live with is that neo-Nazis are still a living force that grows. Like many other cancers its consequences are fated to be tragic.

16
Voices of the Mind

Although retired from academia I'm fit, energetic, and hardworking; I do not regard myself as old. Certainly, I don't feel as if my intellectual life is over. I have come to regard the task at hand as an act of clearing, of unburdening that will allow me to start to build a new life of the mind in my newfound home and city. I want to write a book on the remaking of memory in a world of forgetting. I rage against forgetting. This book would be an essential act of resistance against the technological industrialisation of memory as a force for its erasure. Not only does a loss of memory mean a loss of attention, it also means a loss of control of direction: "If you don't know where you have been, you don't know where you are or where you are going."

McLuhan described television as a cool medium, referring to temperature. No matter what it delivers, irrespective of how near it seems to be, it can never be close. We now live in a world of cool media – emails, texting, Twitter, Zoom and more: the speed of arrival, the condition of appearance, does not close the distance. Once letters were hot. The hand, the pen, the paper, the touch of deliberation, the mark, words of tenderness or criticism could be sensed and felt: they were mediated by touch. None of this survives in the speed of the cool environment of electronic media. Technological mediation and compressed rhetoric evacuate care and reflection and often enable impetuous and sometimes ill-considered words.

The art of the letter is dying/dead and postal services are in decline everywhere. I'm interested in slow words – words that have been carefully thought and spoken or written with care and composed reflectively over a considerable time. A few years ago there was a rush toward things slow – slow food, slow architecture, slow travel and so on. Now "the slow" seems to have lost its fashionable edge.

The logic of the fast world is becoming clear. The faster things move, the more there is to do and the less time *we* all have to do it. This relates to my voices, the voices I hear when I read. It feels like they are from another time. Maybe they are. This feeling is not surprising as in many ways my life has been dominated by words, images and ideas from the past as they occupied my present and directed my future. Speed, accelerated by technology, is destructive of time and is to be feared. Paul Virilio has pointed this out for years, and in particular in relation to war. It's not a new insight. The Sintashta-Arkaim Culture of Eastern Europe and Central Asia knew this in 2100–1800 BCE in their development of the use of war horses. From this moment, the technologies of warfare have not stopped accelerating. Accelerationism has, in fact, become a technological ideology based on accelerating the speed of the arrival of crises and therefore of a path to overcoming them, via a technologically assisted, corporate enabled and commanded phoenix rising from the ashes.

As an exponent of modern warfare, Hitler took the combination of speed, technology and destruction to a whole new level on land, sea and air. This thinking was not just in terms of weapons systems but was applied equally to logistics. For example, Autobahns were not initially built to link cities but to get troops and weapons to the nation's borders as quickly as possible. This was to be able to "hit an enemy hard in massive numbers and very fast." Hitler's blitzkrieg strategy effectively became the fundamental principle of modern conventional 'shock and awe" warfare.

My life has been and still is ruled by work, image, memory and control. Effectively I constructed a regime of self-control and self-censorship as my governing structure. Although what I am doing now can be taken as a breaking out of this condition of order, this does not mean I am liberated from my psychology – it is "me." While I know it's flawed, when I created the structure, I *felt* I had no choice. It allowed me to function. What has changed is that I now know and accept it, but speaking out marks a fundamental change in my life: the moment when

I cleared my past and came to Celle to occupy and go beyond the ruined life I was born into. Celle is not only close to Bergen-Belsen but also the place where my mother was first imprisoned after her arrest. Having a proximity to the place where my life began feels, at least to me, like closing the circle, at least partially.

In reading my words and those of many others on evil, what I hear is a voice that speaks of evil without reference to God. Thus, evil is taken not as an assigned value resting upon a theological normative moral order but as a malevolent force and ontological presence which is of human origin. Hannah Arendt remarked that evil was banal. For her it came in such ordinary guises (memos, instructions, routine orders, purchase orders, slogans and so on). But for me, its banality was beyond this and resides in conduct that is exercised and taken for granted, conduct that is intrinsic to everyday normality. Here is perhaps the most important lesson of the Holocaust *as system* – instrumental and social. How can this banality be explained? I spent a long while thinking about how to answer the question in the context of my mother. I wrote several versions of my conclusion and discarded most of them. Here is the one I settled on.

The essence of evil was not simply lodged in the monstrous acts carried out by my mother and her kindred spirits but in their "habitus" – their inhabited way of thinking, as Pierre Bourdieu describes it. It was in the underlying structure of their thoughts and actions. This structure did not arrive as an integrated whole but as an ideology weaving together doctrinaire education, fostered racism, homophobia, eugenics, and a command structure predicated on the direction of a culture of dehumanisation – all mobilised via a bureaucratic system of implementation deemed banal by Arendt. The Holocaust as habitus, was equally a negation of humanity for those who served it and its victims. As such it was a confluence of cultural induction (training) and inherent individual disposition (trait, flaw, weakness in their being).

Rather than fading and falling with the end of the war, much of this systemic thinking has become incorporated into administrative and labour processes, as a directive of operational structures. What Zygmunt Bauman showed was that the capability of the directive force of the system was such that it had the power to collectivise and repeat horrendously "evil" systematic mass action. History confirms this view, as was seen in the Rwandan genocide in 1994 when Hutu militias killed several hundred thousand Tutsis, and in the Bosnia/Srebrenica massacre of 1992–1995.

As a result of "the system" people act unthinkingly according to *direction, without question.* Uniformity, compliance and efficiency still drive human conduct. People mostly do what the system tells them to do. It is the nature of their job. There is nobody to question, and there is no space of contestation. A higher order of post-industrial mechanised behaviour has arrived. Such instrumentalisation has become economically normative, and can become socio-politically normative too. The contemporary assent to authoritarian populism worldwide is indicative of such a transition.

Thus, the nightmare can arrive, not as an experience of horror that awakens, but unannounced, as the unseen, taken-for-granted every day, as banality. Unthinkingly "just doing," becomes the norm: rewards and career progression are the payoff for compliance. Likewise, the authority of the authoritarian leader to suppress designated "enemies of the people" rests with the lie of acting on behalf of "the people" as a normative consensual fiction. What thereafter becomes evident is complete disorder that has the appearance of order, as a consequence of order stripped of all ethical objectives. The very presence of evil hereafter resides in the "taken-for-granted" exercise of power by a regime and its command of its truth.

Truth is not to be trusted. It is illusive, and has become more so. While it does exist, discerning it has become harder as modes of mediation have proliferated. Not even the voice of the witness is to be trusted. In the Holocaust the only certain truth died with the dead. As Primo Levi wrote in *Survival in Auschwitz*:

We who survived the Camps are not true witnesses. This is an uncomfortable notion that I have gradually come to accept by reading what other survivors have written, including myself, when I re-read my writings after a lapse of years. We, the survivors, are not only a tiny but also an anomalous minority. We are those who, through prevarication, skill or luck, never touched bottom. Those who have, and who have seen the face of the Gorgon, did not return, or returned wordless.

There are things beyond communication. The description of the human being who has lost their humanity can be so described, where what is seen and felt cannot be brought to language. All I am doing here is repeating what so many witnesses to the atrocities of camp life and death have said in various ways.

The witness delivers a certain kind of truth, but it is not the truth of representational correspondences or dispassionate observation. Rather it is the truth of the event and of being there. Thinking about and dealing with the issue of the witness returns me to a voice I still hear, and to my fraught relation to it – the voice of my aunt Helen. She illustrates the problem of the witness. In part she observed the morphing of my mother into the monstrous being she became, as well as witnessing my abandonment. But as I discovered in the history of my relationship with her, seeing does not imply that what has been seen will, or can be, confronted and spoken about.

The pain of the body is unavoidable and revelatory – it discloses the human being who suffers to himself or herself and to others. As Ernst Jünger wrote in *On Pain*, "Tell me your relation to pain and I will tell you who you are!" As such it discloses an unequivocal truth. And pain is a fate that awaits us all. Moreover, it is a value that negates all others. To be in pain is a commonality that dissolves all differences. It does not recognise ethnicity, class, gender, wealth or poverty, though the alleviation of pain, in some but not all circumstances, can be bought if you have the money.

Extreme pain of the mind is another matter (as we have seen), yet in common with pain of the body, it has the ability to overwhelm all else – all other sensations, all other worldly concerns: everything drowns in pain. But then there is the omnipresence of continuous acute pain, a companion, a shadow, immune to all entreaty. The extreme and the continuous both drive the same desire – oblivion.

But there is something else – the presence of the pain of the other in the self – here the witness returns. And here again is the overwhelming of sight by feeling, which renders what is seen unspeakable.

Against this brief reflection on pain, I ask myself: How can shame be understood in terms of pain? To have lived a life in the company of the unspeakable that was *not* seen, forces this question upon me. I saw none of my mother's inhumanity, none of her cruelty. But in relation to her, I feel something that does not mirror my other feelings, including those experienced when presented with extreme human suffering inflicted by nature or by other human beings. As intimated, it feels to me that I carry some of the guilt, some of the responsibility, simply because of the fact that my mother, for all I wish it were not so, was my mother and that she fundamentally refused to acknowledge her own crime against humanity. Without choice, or logic, I was given this obligation. To live with the guilt that she failed to feel was her negative gift to me. Unknowingly, she conceived me to carry this burden. Such a feeling defeats reason, but I know it to be true. This knowledge is totally disconnected from how I think. I have an argument to support the truth. I know I was not responsible for anything my mother did, but I was there, I have "the mark" carried by her cells within me. My argument only carries weight for me.

I doubt that anyone else can really make sense of the way my mother has a presence in my life, and how it is indivisible from my relationship with myself. I am two, not one, and this other, who nobody sees, remains hidden within the walls of the prison house of my mind.

Strange, but whenever I am driving alone, especially on long journeys, I hear myself speaking to her. I cannot silence this inner voice no matter what I do. It defeats all distractions. My voice is never angry. I never moralise, neither do I attempt to discover anything about her motives, mind-set or malformed values. Whatever emotional relations I have, they are not with this person to whom I speak, but rather with their objectified actions (of which I am but one consequence). Actually, I come to the view that she cannot and should not be regarded as an independent subject because, on the one hand, she was inducted and cast into (and from) the Nazi ideological mould, while on the other she seemed to respond to her own impulses and desires without the restraint of a subject able to exercise any form of control. Be it true or false, I have a construct, a picture, a knowledge of what my mother was. What I don't have is any sense of her pre-fascist persona and life. The small and unverified fragments about her family and schooldays were not enough to build an image. What was lacking was memory. I had no memory: she was the unremembered. Her mythology erased all memories. This lack framed what I had to say.

As I spoke to her, I always started with a bunch of questions: "What was your life in Wrechen like? Were you at any time happy at home as a child? When you were young did you like your father? Did he treat you badly? Did he touch you? How much do you remember about your mother? What was your family life like?" Then more pointedly: "Can you recall how your father treated your mother? What were you told when your mother killed herself? How did this action change the way you felt? How did it change the way other people treated you?" Somewhere in the mix of unanswered questions would be the revelation of a moment, a force, an act of wrongdoing that seeded evil.

Sometimes I wondered what she would have said to me if she had not been hanged, and we met at the end of a long prison sentence. It's a perverse scenario to play with, or maybe a play to write. What would the words *sound* like? From reports I read I knew my mother had a soft voice. I know it wasn't cultured, but would there be a hint of feeling? After all she had done, I think not.

In the end, the comfort of silence always arrives to expel curiosity. The same cannot be said for my encounters with the utterance of neo-Nazis. Here is another experience of pain. I want to argue, I want to scream, I want to abuse – but I do nothing. But worse than this is the knowledge, the realisation, that the very disclosure of my existence would for them be a cause for celebration, and this would reduce what I value in my life to rubble. My sense that I made myself into something more than merely my mother's daughter would be ripped from me. These people would contaminate my soul. They would impose the pollutant of hatred, and thereafter I would hate myself for hating – I know what hatred is and from whence it comes. I know that hatred gives birth to the monstrous, and I know that monster.

17

Learning

For all my explanations, I'm still wondering: What have I been doing, writing this story? Where has it taken me? Have I invested all this time in putting these words together purely as an act of self-indulgence? I don't think so. Is it just about me? I don't think so.

In many ways I have found that I don't really know what I know until I write it. It follows that I have learnt a lot about myself from what I have written. At the same time, I'm hopeful that you are learning something more than the details of a troubled life that nonetheless celebrates its attainments and survival. There is not only a dark side to particular individuals, of which my mother was a horrendous example, but also a dark side to humanity itself.

In confronting the horrors of my mother's actions, and in my attempt to live with a genetic and cellular heritage beyond redemption, I learnt something about that inexhaustible object of inquiry: the human condition. I say this after spending a good deal of my life teaching, because no matter how much we think we know, or our level of erudition, and the extent of our technological attainments, humankind still drowns in a sea of ignorance. The most evident sign of this can be seen in our propensity to destroy one another and the environments on which we depend. To move forward I need to backtrack, and then side-track for a few moments.

Is it not strange that people, often great people, with great minds, have been asking questions about the human condition for millennia and still its profound, unquantified mysteries remain? Has what we are essentially changed? Who and what in our differences are we anyway? The names we give things, including ourselves actually mean very little. *Anthropos* (Greek for "human being"); *human* (from the Latin *humanus*, derived from *humus*, "earth"), 人 (Ren, the Chinese pictogram of a human in profile). All such characterisations rest upon a retrospectively applied idea of a being in existence. While this sounds dry, it's important to understand that the image of what has been named, and the values given to it, have become a template to variously form, value and then judge that being so differently named. But the being and the name are not the same thing. In other words, there is something that exists that is other than what has been named, something more original that cannot be reduced to our animal biology. There are variations of "the human" and indigenous self-identities that are other than that which humans designate as human.

Evolution evidences time and change meeting within particular environments so that organisms are subject to specific processes of adaptation. We are aware of the other hominid species that we, in difference, evolved from. *Homo sapiens* evolved incrementally from and beyond our progenitors. Most dramatically in our evolutionary development, the hominid brain increased dramatically in size by over thirty percent from our most primitive origins over hundreds of thousands of years to the moment our species appeared about 160,000 years ago. Our bodies changed far less significantly. What we have little sense of, however, is the extent of what remained the same.

What is clear, and what one can say here, is that humankind is not secure. According to circumstances, as a species we can fragment, progress or regress. While humans and their hominid others have an enormous capacity for learning, there is also an innate disposition, a refusal, a space of closure, towards unlearning. Under most circumstances the power of inculcation, pedagogic exposure and social mores acts to suppress this disposition.

Thomas Hobbes saw civil society, the law and politics as the means by which humankind's animal nature, "red in tooth and claw," could be held in check. In many respects the Enlightenment idealistically elevated reason as the agency and guiding power that could oversee this projected progression of human civilisation. But the Third Reich, in the modern world, burst this illusory bubble. It showed how reason could be employed in the service of unreason and that the power of the intellect was and is insufficient to tame the irrational seed within it.

While our focus on the irrational has veered toward the dark side it also brings positive qualities to life and being, including our aesthetic and emotional responses to music, dance, the visual arts, the natural environment, and all things sensual. Although reason has played a major part in the making of the modern mind, its limitation and insufficiency are now increasingly becoming recognised.

In telling my story, as someone whose past has colonised and directed so much of their future, the significance of what I have been saying goes beyond me and the afterlife of my mother. Wider-than-personal issues have passed through me, and my history exposes this movement. Not least among these issues was the inheritance of negation that some of my generation experienced. Put simply, the bequest of a parent/parents who gave their child nothing except a disabling psychological burden to carry throughout their life was almost, and in some cases totally, unbearable.

 I have been playing a double game with myself, which in truth I only discovered on reflection: I have been concealing as I reveal. Though I am damaged goods, I am also proud I managed to survive and hold my demons at bay. Without the resilience and determination that I somehow created and drew on, I believe that this would not have happened. I would have been a wreck, a drunk, a drug addict or dead. From this understanding I again come back to the question: what have I learnt? A number of things stand out for me.

We modern human beings are not what we appear to be. Our attributes are plural – clearly, we are not all the same, we don't all occupy the same cosmology, culture or ideology. Nonetheless most of us present ourselves to ourselves as if we are in charge of our lives at least to some degree. Many of us would claim, in some form or other, to be an independent conscious being with a will of our own. But this is not how it is. So often we are not in the driving seat of our lives. So often others, circumstances, systems, communication structures and cultures directly or indirectly determine our thoughts, actions and desires. History stamps on us and sometimes squashes us. This is often underpinned by economic or social situations, but sometimes evil forces call the shots. Painfully I learnt that such evil can have a beautiful face; it can glitter, and be an object of admiration.

We live in a mist, so we don't see the world around us clearly. This is not because there is something wrong with our vision but with our minds. As Plato pointed out in *The Republic* millennia ago: "We see with our mind, not our eyes." Our eyes are mere optical instruments that relay information to our brain to be made sense of by what we already know. The mist of our minds then produces an interpretative inadequacy. We are always constrained by the limits of our knowledge. And our mode of knowing is always formed out of a specific moment of the world within the world that we humans have created. Such knowledge never provides a clear means to see the inter-relational complexity of the world. Once I had an argument with Christopher over nature. He could not accept that it was only something we observe and see, but rather a perceptual frame that is intrinsic to our very being: we are part of it. We see nature via the idea of "nature." The ideal nature is in fact an abstraction that is not reducible to a historically and culturally relative category of human invention. For us there is no outside, and therefore we can never observe nature other than by looking from inside. The objectification of nature is a conceit.

What we do know is that our perception of the world cannot be separated from the language that we use. As Ludwig Wittgenstein pointed out, "The limits of my language are the limits of my world." Effectively, every language has its own construction of reality. By implication, while all of humanity physically lives in the same world, perceptually, different language groups create and occupy different worlds.

Yet for all the cultural differences of humanity, so much of what we are remains the same. What this recognises is that, at its basic level, biologically we remain animals, and very dangerous ones. In this context culture and civilisation are a veneer that, as we have seen, often turns out to be thin and fragile. Yet many cultures seem to be under the impression that they are firm and secure and that their animality is behind them in some distant past. Not true. Such thinking fails to recognise that human beings are part of nature – we are part of what we claim to observe. Equally this is a failure to recognise the form of our presence in the natural and unnatural (that is, constructed) condition of our fate.

I really do not think that these things that I have learnt are hard to understand. Yet the fact is that, in general, they do not seem to be at the core of the conflict, discrimination and hatred within the world.

18

The Good

Moral and ethical concern with "the good" travels back across the entire history of philosophy and directly links to the theological and culturally relative question of evil. Whereas all cultures have a concept that equates to evil, and define good entities as being bountiful, wholesome, offering pleasure and rewards and so on, "the good" is predicated on a moral philosophy.

It is claimed that there are a set of seven rules that all cultures share: help your family – this can be claimed to be true, with the qualification that what a family is cannot be viewed as culturally uniform; help your group – social atomisation and individuation means that not everyone has a group; return favours – this implies a level of social functionality that not all individuals have; be brave – too relativistic to be meaningful (an eight year old being brave when going to the dentist has nothing in common with an eighteen year old going to war); defer to superiors – this depends on who the superiors are, who defines them, and in what context; divide resources fairly – in a world of inequity this claim is hollow; and respect others' property – many do not have property. Notwithstanding such claims, in the diversity of our species' modes of being there is no normative value of the good. While all cultures posit things as good, not all cultures articulate it as a moral philosophy.

What interests me now is how to think futurally. How is it possible to live in the material present of our troubled world and act so as to have positive effects? A big question. It shifts the evaluation of what is good from subjective and relative moral judgements to something able to be seen and empirically evaluated at the level of "the good life", which is taken to mean good for the self and for the well-being of all upon which life depends.

This shift of emphasis to the material does not require any kind of radical shift into the unknown: the means of evaluation is already present, albeit reflected in an underdeveloped worldly engagement. An easy example to illustrate this claim is food: good food has measurable qualities based on high nutritional value and correlates with demographic markers of human health. Good food does good and the form and effect of this good can be described – not via a gourmet's espousal of good (i.e., luxurious and expensive) food and drink – but in terms of the original Epicurean understanding. According to Epicurean philosophy, good food is that which increases the well-being of the self and is produced in a way that cares for the environment from which the food comes, in the context of a culture where one lives modestly, gains an understanding of the world, and constrains one's desires.

Could not this thinking be generalised to define "the good" as being anything that sustains life in all its forms and in all its environments, and frees it from bad (or evil) substances or actions that would or could harm its well-being? This is easy to contemplate, but it is hard to turn thought of "the good" into the operative frameworks of social, civil, economic and political action. It's an enormous challenge that requires "the good" to be disentangled from the discourses of morality, the rhetoric of marketing, hedonism, and subjectivism projected as an objective claim.

At one level this is obvious. But moving from abstraction to enacting "the good" in reality is another matter that requires our return to the mobilisation, reclaiming and grounding of reason in "the good." The "good" so framed implies that the qualitative condition of life in general is secured beyond mere existence. In this context reason has to be decoupled from its service to the irrational. War is a case in point: whereas rational means are created to wage it, the destruction it delivers to environments, bodies, families, cultures and minds is completely irrational. We know this, yet we falter in action. I have strived to carry out such a decoupling in my life.

I don't want to lose sight of where all these thoughts originated. My intention has not been to write a book of political philosophy, nor am I trying to right the ills of the world. Rather I am trying to deal with the fact that I am a child of the irrational. I have lived my life, day in day out, in the midst of a struggle between the irrational and reason, with the forces of my mind and my mother's physical and mental presence in and upon me.

I am now conscious that the irrationality of my mother was not totally a product of her own making. As a mentally unstable person, she was seduced by an idea and an image, as were many millions of others, but her surrender to the inherent unreason of these tropes, and to her own perverse desires, was absolute. The skill of the shaman, the messianic tyrant, transformed an insane and irrational analysis of a problem into a simple, rational and attractive solution (a final solution) for her and a whole nation.

Over a lifetime of study and thought, my view of the nature of evil (as malevolent intent) has changed. I believe evil is changing from a manifestation of human nastiness to an embodied quality of certain malevolent technologies produced by the auto-destructive liberation of the agency of instrumentalism. The evil demons of mind, image, and directive give rise to destruction as the effective negative endpoint of all unchecked human creation. In other words, humanity stands to destroy itself by allowing uncontrolled instrumentalism free rein through a technology of unlimited excess.

The making of more without limit is excess, and excess so understood at a planetary level can be called evil, for it is the path to extinction. The Holocaust also delivered a message of excess, which sadly, in large part, went unheard. In both cases the issue is excess as unrestrained conduct not just of individuals and regimes, but also at the level of world making (the world of accelerated technological extraction, production and consumption) imposing a made world on the given world.

The essence of Nazism was an ideology directing the irrational mobilisation of instrumental reason as a system of administration, via a directive leadership centred on the shaman and the interpolative power of ideology. But power has seeped away from both misguided and guided control. Technology is becoming an independent power.

In sum, looking back and toward the future, I unreservedly view the domain of technology as becoming malevolent – as a burgeoning inanimate evil. As technological beings, any sense that we are in control of technology has gone; anyone who still believes humans control technology is, in my view, naïve. Against this negative picture of technology, how do I now understand "the good" as a material order (rather than a moral order)? Well, it is anything that sustains life free from any substances or actions that would or could harm human health and well-being, together with all those other forms of life and the environments upon which life depends. Technology hereafter becomes measured against this proposition as a basis of normative judgement. The counter idealism of this position is basic, and unless this position becomes dominant, we human beings, as finite beings, will not survive. Technology so viewed cannot be seen as a means of dealing with threats to the environment we all depend upon. Indivisibly, and in numerous ways, it is a cause of its destruction, and our understandings of these causalities remain limited.

A few months before I moved to Celle, my friend Karen came to visit on her way to perform at a concert in Berlin. We stayed up into the early hours of Sunday morning talking and arguing about belief. A couple of themes from this lively and enjoyable conversation have stayed with me. The first was the need to believe. We agreed that the need to believe, grounded in some form of good, could actually be significant, so, what to believe? Beliefs held in common bring people together. As anthropologists have pointed out, belief is at the very basis of community. Its loss in the modern, and especially the Western secular, world is directly connected to the breakdown of community. The need to believe is materialised in the need for community (human beings depend on each other; we exist within a social ecology and, as such, are social animals).

This led to another question we spent time talking about: "What can we believe in now, that will reconstitute the community?" We realised belief had to relate to something real; it could not simply be invented. It had to have substance – notions like "belief in ourselves" or "in the future" were too flaky. In the end we settled on "belief in culture sustaining life " and "community sustaining culture."

This question went full circle and became more contentious when we arrived at the contradiction between faith and reason. For me faith is irrational – it is an act of believing without any grounds for belief. It takes what is posited on trust. For Karen the need for faith outweighed the problem of its lack of a foundation in reason. We were able to agree that the non-rational can establish a shared understanding that enables social lives to function (here we connect back to belief). What proved harder to agree on was the contradictory movement between unreason and fatalism on the one hand and reason and rational decision-making on the other. For example, in Islam, a situation can arise when reason is applied to deliver an end result that, irrespective of whether it succeeds or fails, is not attributed to the application of reason but rather to "the will of Allah."

Finally, we both agreed that this dichotomy was not a product of a particular religion, but was inherent in our being: to varying degrees, every human being glides between reason and the irrational, often in almost the same instant. We cannot claim to be completely rational.

After trying to make sense of "the good", I was struck by how superficial almost all discussions about it are, based as they are on judgments underscored by belief in normative values that go unexamined. As for the bad, discussions about it can be just as vacuous; empirically there can be plenty of evidence in plain sight for its existence, but equally it can hide. Beauty can conceal evil.

19

The End

A lot has changed for me since I started writing this memoir. I do not see my mother or myself as I once did. I'm pleased I have found answers to some of my questions, and accepted that there are others where the quest is futile. The answers lie with the dead.

So here I am in my apartment, having come to the end of my exorcism. Am I now free? No. My mother ensured that freedom could never be. But having reflected upon my life it appears before me with a degree of legibility that it never had before. I now know that the load to be carried feels lighter. Perhaps this means I can journey forward in a new way. Time will tell. Finally, I close with a confession and a symbolic act.

Gerda is my real name but Schwab is not. I have also changed the names of other people, and while I did teach at a university in the northeast of the US, it was not Stony Brook. So, I remain concealed in my exposure. I do this no longer because of a fear of being seen, or out of shame. Rather it has become the only way I can be. When I rise from my chair I will remove and retire my beloved old suitcase to a shelf of its own in a cupboard in my hall. I am now in the world from which it was transported.

Acknowledgements

First, I want to especially thank D Wood for her critical reading and insights, editorial acumen and the resulting to improvements of the text and to her generosity. As always Anne-Marie Willis has made numerous perceptive comments, constructive criticism and given unfailing support. I would also like to thank Eleni Kalantidou for her words of encouragement.

Research Notes

With the exception of: *Der Spiegel*, 'Die Akte Auschwitz, ' 35/August (2014), and Frances Cronin, 'Nazi legacy: The troubled descendants' *BBC New Magazine* 23 May (2012). I am not going to list the huge number of newspapers, magazines and academic journals I have read. There are a number key works consulted, with three mentioned in passing in the text that have been important. These are, Elie Wiesel, *Night* (1960); Primo Levi, *Survival at Auschwitz* (1959), Zygmunt Bauman, *Modernity and the Holocaust* (1989). A large number of works on philosophy and psychology were consulted, but not directly cited. Archival material of particular note were: Jewish Virtual library (https://www.jewishvirtuallibtary.org) and *The Holocaust Encyclopedia* (https://www.ushmm.org), both were important sources of information. *Law Reports of Trials of War Criminals, The United Nations War Crimes Commission*, HMSO, London, 1947 (especially Volume II, Case No 10, The Belsen Trial) was a key text. In 1961 Hannah Arendt attended the Adolf Eichmann trial in Jerusalem as a reporter for *The New Yorker* in November 1962. This resulted in Eichmann in Jerusalem (1963) where she addressed the issue of 'the banality of evil' - a concept of significance to this text, and in the subsequent book based on this material. Emmanuel Levinas's essay on 'Transcendence and Evil in his *Collection of Philosophical Papers* (1987) was important. An article by Steve Morris in the *Guardian* in May 2012 presented an analysis of Hitler's mental state, drawn up by British intelligence in 1942, uncovered by a Cambridge University researcher, Scott Anthony, who found a report commissioned by the social scientist Mark Abrams, a pioneer of market research and opinion polling. Abrams worked in the psychological warfare division of the allied expeditionary force during the second world war. Abrams's report proved to be of great interest. Other works that were consulted, included Jean Baudrillard, "The Evil Demon of Images." (1984), Ilya Ehrenburg and Vasily Grossman. *The Complete Black Book of Russian Jewry* (2003), Raul Hilberg, *The Destruction of the European Jews* (1961), Ernst Jünger, *On Pain* (2008), and Robert Martone's article, "Scientists Discover Children's Cells Living in Mothers' Brains." *Scientific American*, 4 December (2012).

Milton Keynes UK
Ingram Content Group UK Ltd.
UKHW021949130524
442669UK00002B/27

9 781804 413791